BREAKING THE BLUE WALL

C.S.U. - Criminal Justice Department.
Thank you for supporting
the cause!

BREAKING

—THE—

BLUE WALL

One Man's War Against Police Corruption

JUSTIN HOPSON

WESTBOW
P R E S S
A DIVISION OF THOMAS NELSON

WestBow Press books may be ordered through booksellers or by contacting:

WestBow Press
A Division of Thomas Nelson
1663 Liberty Drive
Bloomington, IN 47403
www.westbowpress.com
1-(866) 928-1240

ISBN: 978-1-4497-0378-3 (sc)
ISBN: 978-1-4497-0379-0 (dj)
ISBN: 978-1-4497-0377-6 (ebk)

Library of Congress Control Number: 2010932298

Printed in the United States of America

WestBow Press rev. date: 11/21/2011

CONTENTS

Acknowledgements

First and foremost, all glory to God, my Shepard. A deep thanks to my wife who is the wind in my sails and inspiration...Such a blessing. I am eternally grateful to my children and their gift of love - thank you for seeing in yourself what you see in me. Heartfelt thanks and love to my mother who has been my emotional backbone. Special thanks to the Oliva family, Funk family, Blankenship family, and Catenella family for being so supportive. Gratitude goes to the collaborative efforts of Rob Suggs, for being part of the marrow of this book.

I'd like to recognize Frank "Paco" Serpico (retired NYPD), Dr. Susan Lipkins (psychologist), and Bill Buckman (attorney) for their resounding influence. To every journalist who has covered this story, kudos to you. Last but not least, I'd like to thank my true friends and unforgettable foes that contributed to my cause. Any book eight years in the making has blood, sweat, and tears behind it. It's truly an honor to be able to share my journey with each of you!

Disclaimer

This book, in its entirety, is a fact-based personal account, with the sole exception of altered names in a few cases to protect personal privacy. All copy-written material has been permitted. All facts, evidence, and testimony can be verified through **Hopson v. State of New Jersey**, et al (Case#1:03-cv-5817).

Chapter 1:

Fateful Night on a Moonlit Road

Night came again, and with it the fear.

Evening had once been a peaceful time for me, a few hours to wind down after a healthy day's work. Now my life was considerably different. The quiet was unsettling, the little noises even worse. The brief glint of a headlight off the window glass quickened my pulse. The rustling of a twig or a tree could be nothing at all, or something for worry.

I spent my time listening and waiting these days. But for whom or what?

Somebody had told me, "Just because you're paranoid doesn't mean they're not out to get you." I think it was meant as a joke.

Who could really say whether this was paranoia? The assaults I had suffered were real enough. So were the verbal threats, the anonymous notes, and those guys with their eyes fixed on me, whispering behind my back. At night my fears intensified, watching a police cruiser shine its spotlight on my home and minutes later answering my telephone only to hear the heavy breathing of an unknown caller. It was all intended to provoke exactly what I was feeling right now; all intended to bully me into backing down.

How far was I willing to go? How much of this before I fell into line and behaved myself, or alternatively surrendered and found some other line of work?

Something had to give. That was pretty clear, I thought, glancing down at the gun in my hand. Had I really taken to arming myself around my own home? This was no way to live. It seemed to me that I was the last guy who would have been voted "Most Likely to Take On the Establishment"; for that matter, the last guy you'd expect to be put on meds for depression—particularly in my twenties, the prime of life.

I had wanted nothing more than to quietly do my job, to protect and to serve the public.

I thought about the crowd with whom I grew up, the old friends. They were out there somewhere, taking life the way you're supposed to do at our age. They had parties, they went boating or skiing or camping, they married and had kids. As for me, I couldn't even keep a girlfriend. My ongoing tension and mood swings had scared the last of them away.

So there it was, me against the world. Not that I didn't have support in some sense—there were channels and authorities that had my back, at least up to a point. I was working through the system, and my charges were being taken seriously. But at the end of the day, or at the beginning of the night, those channels and authorities went home. They weren't here to help me listen for footsteps or watch for headlights.

I thought about that, clinched my teeth one more time, and recalled the unlikely chain of events that brought me to this crossroad.

I had pursued my dream. Being a New Jersey State Trooper was the destiny I had elected for myself from grade school onward. This was what I wanted to do with my life.

My dad, a retired federal law enforcement agent, gave me a taste of the career he found satisfying. He engraved into my soul the concepts of integrity, of maintaining the common good—in the simplest terms, of doing what is right. Sure, those are basic American values, the stuff we all learn at home, at school, and at church. But my dad was out there seeing that it was done, stepping up to be responsible for a better community and world.

I wanted more than anything to follow in his footsteps. I hurried through my teenage years with an imagination enflamed by TV cop shows, crime movies, and daily episodes from the life of my father who had a propensity for storytelling.

I did slow down long enough for a college education and even grad school. Maybe that made me a little different from other guys in my field. However, one could say that, all those studies worked towards an end goal of getting a career in law enforcement and doing everything I could with the opportunity.

When my education was complete, I found myself in my mid-twenties with a choice between the California Highway Patrol and the New Jersey State Police. West Coast or East Coast, Golden State or Garden State? My head said, "Go west, young man," but my heart told me to stay home, where I could remain rooted with my family and friends.

In September of 2001—a big week in my life and, in tragic ways, that of our nation—I entered the police academy to train for the New Jersey State Police. The lieutenant in the recruiting office was friendly and encouraging. He also warned me that I'd better be ready for a twenty-three week, boot camp experience. It would be like enlisting in a branch of military service. I had an idea of what lay ahead, and I took it seriously, running, boxing, and weightlifting the days away until my time came.

There was a reading requirement, too: a book on police ethics and the value system of American law enforcement. The book made plenty of sense to me. If anything, those things went without saying; law enforcement was all about doing the right thing. I was ready for a lifelong commitment as a public servant, prepared for the responsibility of protecting citizens and enforcing the law regardless of race, sex, or creed.

As I'd been brought up, that's how we do things in America.

Even with all my measures, there was no way to be thoroughly prepared for the challenges of police training at the academy. It was a rigorous camp drawn from military traditions, where the soft civilian is broken down and recreated as a finely-honed, disciplined soldier ready to follow orders. That was fine with me. I wanted to be the best, and I was grateful that our state demanded high standards for its officers. Frankly, I was excited about measuring myself against my fellow recruits.

The New Jersey State Police Academy is located in Sea Girt, a little borough near the southeast corner of the state. For nearly six months, we checked in at six in the morning Monday and checked out on Friday at six in the evening. Each day began with military drill and the raising of the colors. We ran on the New Jersey beaches at mid-winter while drill instructors barked away, working up to five miles at an eight-minute pace. We pummeled each other to the floor in self-defense classes and in the boxing ring, where I learned to hold my own against fellow recruits. We marched until we wore out the soles of our boots on the cold cement, just as if we were preparing to invade Delaware. There were sixty hours of firearms instructions, with firing range testing, and twenty-one hours of defensive driving instruction. It was a career's worth of training packed into a few months.

Academy Marching Drill

My academic background had prepared me for the classroom portion. Again, the great thrust of it went without saying, in my opinion: the profound responsibility of enforcing the law courteously and constitutionally. The core values of the New Jersey State Police are honor, duty, and fidelity.

Then there were the rigid requirements in the little things: folding clothing, mopping floors, cleaning toilets, shining shoes, proper haircut and appearance. I could see the value of military training, and why young men and women emerged with a discipline that guided them through the rest of their lives. Even if I wasn't heading for a career in law enforcement, I would have been a better man for any life pursuit, having experienced this half-year of being sculpted into a soldier.

Best of all, I was going to get to the end of it. I was going to escape the barking drill instructors, the water skills testing, the running, the marching, the fighting, and the studying—and begin my life work.

The graduation ceremony was the proud day for which everyone waits. We paraded in our electric blue uniforms trimmed with gold and our fitted blue hats. The uniforms have changed very little since 1921, when Colonel H. Norman Schwarzkopf, police superintendent, deployed the first eighty-one New Jersey State Troopers on horseback and motorcycle.

Author's Academy Graduation

Those unique uniforms are another cherished point of pride and tradition. We received our badges and shook the governor's hand. It was Trooper Cole, a popular veteran in the State Police, who presented my prized badge.

I had made it; I was ready to live the dream of my youth, serving my state in law enforcement. I was a raw rookie, wondering how soon the real adventures would begin. The answer was eleven days.

It felt good to be in uniform and on duty. I had earned my badge, but now it was time to pay my dues. According to routine, I would ride on patrol with a more experienced officer, keep my mouth shut as much as possible, and observe what happens in a typical day.

For the first few days, things couldn't have been quieter. We issued a speeding ticket here and wrote up an accident report there. Daytime duty generally wasn't the stuff of prime time television. After about a week, however, I got my first taste of the nightshift. I looked forward to some new learning experiences. As everyone knows, after the sun goes down and the bars open, trouble is more likely to make itself known. I was riding with Trooper Patrick Cole, the same officer who had presented my badge at graduation. I didn't know him well, of course, but I looked up to him as a veteran on the force. I was eager to learn what he had to teach.

We were patrolling a small rural town, the kind of highway dotted by trailer parks alternating with stretches of pine trees. It was a cold and crisp evening lit by a clear moon; the world seemed to have gone off to bed as we drove along and monitored the radio dispatch. Still, it was Saturday night, and we remained alert.

Fairly late in the evening, we came to a stop sign at an intersection and began to slow to a stop. Crossing in front of us was a red, four-door sedan. As we came closer, our headlights revealed the interior of the car: a teenage white male at the wheel and a white female passenger.

As the car cautiously came around and passed us, I caught sight of a third passenger. This one was a blonde young lady seated directly behind the driver. She and I made eye contact. As a matter of fact, all the passengers had that "deer-in-the-headlights" look in their eyes, wishing to be invisible. Most important from our perspective, the vehicle's registration was expired.

Without a word, Trooper Cole twisted the wheel of the patrol car and followed the red car. I loosened my seat belt and prepared to assist Trooper Cole in handling whatever came up with the teenagers we were pursuing. For just a moment, the red car disappeared after cresting a hill. It couldn't have gone far, of course, and we picked it up shortly. The driver had made a quick turn into a trailer park that was unlit. When we caught up, the sedan was parked with its headlights off. Clearly the driver was desperately eager to avoid being pulled over—which, of course, is usually a sign that the situation calls for closer scrutiny.

Trooper Cole pulled our patrol car to the proper distance behind the red vehicle and parked. There we sat on a dirt road in a heavily wooded area. Cole turned on our overhead lights, prepped the dashboard mobile video camera and microphone, while notifying the dispatcher that we were on a motor vehicle stop.

As this was happening, the two young women began to approach us from the sedan. Trooper Cole pushed his hat into place and commanded them to go back to their vehicle and wait inside.

I climbed out and walked to the rear of the red sedan, as I'd been trained to do. The seasoned veteran, Trooper Cole in this case, had the job of taking the lead and interviewing the driver. My role was to stand at his flank, check out the interior with my flashlight, and be ready for anything unexpected. Already there was a question in my mind: *Where is the male driver?*

He was the key player here. He was the one operating the vehicle and therefore responsible for any laws that were being broken. Yet it was the blonde who was now sitting behind the wheel. I was sure Trooper Cole had noticed the discrepancy and would demand the whereabouts of the driver. I beamed my flashlight around the area, but the vanishing chauffer was nowhere to be found. He turned out to be invisible after all.

Trooper Cole was interviewing the blonde, identified in this book as "Krista." I approached the car and shined my light into its interior, revealing a few empty beer bottles strewn here and there. I pointed them out to Cole, who had finished his preliminary questions: "Where are you going? May I see your driver's license and registration?" and so on. He now asked Krista to step out of the car.

As she emerged from the vehicle for the second time, I could see that she was nervous. She was also intoxicated, which was not against the law, as long as she was merely a passenger. I had seen with my own eyes that she hadn't been driving, regardless of where she had re-seated herself. Krista had been in the back seat, directly behind the male driver who had apparently taken flight on foot.

Cole began the standard series of field sobriety tests. For the first time in my eleven-day apprenticeship as a New Jersey State Trooper, I had an important question to ask. Why were we doing this? The girl was a passenger. But this was not the moment for verbalizing my question. I did what rookies do—kept my mouth shut and left the matter to my superior officer.

Krista didn't excel at her test. She couldn't lift her leg for thirty seconds. She couldn't deliver a clear recitation of the alphabet. Trooper Cole looked her in the eye and said, "You're under arrest for driving under the influence." He commanded Krista to turn around and place her hands behind her back.

"I wasn't driving the damn car!" shouted Krista. She had done everything asked of her, but this wasn't the outcome she seemed to be expecting. Now she began to panic.

In response to her protests, Cole made a grab for her wrist to snap a handcuff in place. But Krista had just enough reflexive coordination left to dodge and run. And just like that, our questionable suspect was headed for the woods, with two trained, well-conditioned and sober state troopers in pursuit. There was only one way that could end; it was Cole who tripped Krista, sending her tumbling.

"It wasn't me! I wasn't driving!" she reiterated, waving her arms as if a movie were being filmed, and the scene needed to be reshot. "Get the hell off of me!" Cole loomed over her, threatening her with a can of pepper spray.

I have to admit, I shared Krista's feeling that somehow we had found ourselves in a bad cop movie. I looked incredulously at Cole, the respected officer who had presented my badge, with disbelief. He was not only violating the law, but also doing it in front of a brand new trainee fresh out of the academy. He had no idea how I might respond. This made no sense at all.

Why was this a big deal? Compared to the things you might see in a "bad cop" movie—officers taking drug money, accepting bribes and the like—arresting the wrong teenager might seem trivial. I don't see it that way at all. At the very foundation of American law, in the Fourth Amendment to our Constitution, lies the idea of *probable cause*—the right of the people to be secure in their persons, houses, papers, and effects against unreasonable searches and seizures. Until this night, I took that idea for granted. Not even a rookie needed to learn when an arrest was unlawful. We had probable cause to pull the car over and deal with lapsed automobile registration. We didn't have it for detaining a drunken passenger.

But frankly, that's Cop 101. It was almost like some bizarrely elaborate test of my integrity, to see if I was man enough to stand up to a rogue cop, if things came to that. That "conspiracy theory" was more than unlikely, of course. I was new, but I wasn't naïve enough to be ignorant of the fact that things like this went on—even in training situations, even among the proud New Jersey State Police, even at the hands of "respectable" officers, those who were held before us as examples.

My head was spinning. What was I going to do?

I wasn't sure, but Krista had made her decision. She knew that all bets were off, and she had no choice but to cooperate—though she didn't intend to go quietly. She submitted to the cuffs and to being placed in the backseat of the patrol car, complaining all the while. Cole and I walked back toward the red sedan, which still held a terrified occupant. The other young woman, who turned out to be the car's actual owner, was sitting in the front passenger seat, watching the festivities through the rear-view mirror. She was now ordered out and into the backseat of our patrol car, where she would join her friend. I looked at the two of them as I was shutting their door—the look of complete disbelief on their faces. The shock was stronger than the booze; they were nearly scared sober by this point.

I was scared, too. I was involved in a process that was diametrically opposed to everything I had been taught, everything I believed, everything my father had drummed into me about doing the right thing. I hadn't waited all my life to quickly get involved in a routine violation of civil rights.

Trooper Cole was in firm control of events by now, for better or for worse. He showed no indication of anything being amiss in his handling of things. He now pointed me back toward the red sedan. It was my job to search the interior compartments of the vehicle incidental to the arrest. I shuffled through the center console, a few loose papers, the door compartments, between the seat cushions, and anywhere I might find drug paraphernalia. Nothing was there— including, strangely enough, the car keys. Like the driver, they couldn't be accounted for.

Cole hadn't missed this fact, and he ordered me to keep looking under the seat and floor mat. Finally I confirmed to him that the keys weren't there.

Cole was irritated. "We know where they are," he commented. "In the pants pocket of the guy who was driving, and ditched."

He walked back to the rear passenger side of the patrol car and confronted Krista. "Who's the driver?" he asked her.

The girls started talking rapidly. "They ran!" "We don't know where they went!"

It turned out there were not one but two males unaccounted for. One had slipped my notice; it wasn't clear whether Cole had seen him or not. "What are their names?" demanded Cole.

"We just met them! Hooked up at a party. We didn't get their names . . ."

In a quiet way, a crucial moment had just passed. By acknowledging a male driver, Trooper Cole was verbally confirming that he was making an unlawful arrest. Without the driver, there was absolutely no charge to pin upon these women, other than the lapsed automobile registration.

The whole scene had become surreal from my vantage point. At what point was I supposed to speak up? I was completely unprepared. It had never occurred to me that I might be in a situation like this, with the ink on my criminal justice certificate barely dry.

I held my tongue for the time being and assisted Cole in securing the car. Soon a tow truck would be on the scene to impound it. Then we returned to the patrol car. As we prepared to take the two women to the station, Krista's anger reasserted itself. She began kicking the protective divider in sheer rage and frustration. Cole whirled around, and I expected him to warn the blonde to get a grip on her emotions and her feet. Instead, he unplugged the standard microphone. It had been activated since we stopped, and it was recording everything that transpired. Then he began another round of interrogation: *Who was the driver? What do you know about these guys? Describe them!*

How many times have I relived the situation—this time, in my imagination, having the presence of mind to snap cuffs on Cole and call for support? I just wasn't ready to pull off something that bold, though it would absolutely have been the correct course of action.

Instead, I did as I was told; I climbed out of the car, walked up the road to the highway, and watched for the tow. Meanwhile, Cole relentlessly shouted questions at the young women in an effort to wear them down and get the information he wanted.

I felt the anxiety welling up in my chest. My thoughts were jumbled as I walked the two blocks, waved down the tow truck, and pointed it back toward the sedan. When I got back to the patrol car, nothing had changed. Krista was still kicking the divider, still shouting, "I wasn't driving the damn car and you know it! This is crazy!"

As Cole started the car and pulled onto the road, he re-plugged the microphone and set his course for the State Police barracks. The ride was quiet. At that point, I began to arrive at some vague idea of a personal strategy. I was going to do everything in my power to exonerate the two young women in the back seat of this patrol car. I didn't know what the price of that decision might be, but I intended to be steadfast in my resolution to do the right thing.

Any other plan would have meant that the dream career I'd pursued for most of my life was nothing but an illusion.

Chapter 2:

Aftermath

At the barracks, we did the paperwork and processed the two women for the violation of driving under the influence. Krista was also charged with obstruction of justice for attempting to flee.

I took Krista's picture and began fingerprinting her. As I did so, I made eye contact for the first time since her car first crossed our path. "Are you okay?" I asked though it was clear from looking at her that she was anything but okay.

"No, I'm not," she said. "I don't know what I'm doing here."

Doing my best to offer some token of reassurance I said, "Try not to worry. It's all going to work out all right. We'll have you out of custody before you know it."

I saw Krista watching me uncertainly. Why was this trooper more human than the other one? "Why should you care one way or the other?" she asked.

I offered a smile and told her that was my job.

Over the next hour, several thousand dollars of fines were levied; a court date was set. There was no way these two women could easily handle the dollar figures demanded. Their dress, their speech, and their side of town made it likely that the fines would be enough to take a terrible toll on their lives. This fact added to my indignation over the arrest—thousands of dollars to pay for a crime that never happened. It would also be a black mark on their public record. Eventually the two were released from custody to a friend.

As the end of the shift finally approached, Trooper Cole gave me new instructions. He wanted me to start writing the drunk driving report according to the "facts" as he dictated them. I felt myself sinking deeper into this mire of misconduct—I was now being required to support his unlawfulness by the act of my typing and the affixing of my signature. It was obvious the report was going to be issued one way or the other; add "false report" to the evening's list of transgressions.

The fact of the matter was that the only laws broken here were by the police, not the detainees.

I finished typing and headed to the locker room. As I quietly undressed from my uniform and into my civilian attire, Cole walked in, stood nearby, and began talking to some of his buddies. "You should have seen these scumbags who tried to run tonight," he said. I didn't look up, not wanting to be a part of his enjoyment of the tale. I secured my gun and equipment and prepared to leave as Cole went on recounting the incident. *Is this standard procedure for him?* I wondered. *Does it not bother him at all what he's done?* This was certainly how it appeared. My guess was that his past held a long list of innocent citizens who were locked up, paid unjust fines, and had fictional crimes on their records.

I did not sign up for any of this, I thought. I was smoldering as I walked out of the locker room. A hand touched my shoulder—it was Cole. "Good job tonight," he said.

"Yes sir," I said in a non-committal fashion, avoiding his eyes.

I have no idea how I got home that evening. I suppose my body was on autopilot. My mind wasn't in the driver's seat, but filled with frantic, conflicting thoughts about what I should have or could have done—and what I should do or could do now.

The sun was coming up, and some part of me found morning to be a hopeful sight. Everything looked better in the early light, right? The warmth felt good on my face, but that face didn't look good in the rearview mirror; I seemed to have added a few years overnight. I was wired and tired, equally excited and exhausted. I walked into the kitchen of our condominium and said hello to my roommate. I wasn't sure how much I could tell him about the evening's events. Why get him involved? He was a fellow trooper and academy classmate, which meant that he would understand my predicament. On the other hand, I really didn't want him to be privy to the situation. Most of all, why get him involved in the mess that awaited me?

I kept a poker face and hurried into my bedroom, where I knew I could grab a phone and talk to the one person whose advice would really matter: my father. He was instrumental in me becoming a state trooper and had the experience to know how to handle something like this.

It was the end of a long day for me, but it was a fresh new one for my father. I started from the beginning and gave him all the details. I figured I knew him well enough, after all these years, to anticipate his advice: *Report the training officer's misconduct to a superior, Justin.* Hearing my father say this would embolden me, reassure me that I was doing the right thing.

After quietly hearing me out, I was shocked by how he actually responded, "Justin, don't make any waves," he said. "You don't want to piss those guys off, believe me. My advice to you is to go along to get along."

For a second I was speechless, knocked for a loop by his stance. He had taught me integrity and honesty. But he was also a dad who kept my safety and wellbeing paramount. I hadn't yet figured that into the equation.

"Come on, are you serious?" I asked. "Go along to get along? This is someone's life we're talking about. This is against everything . . ."

"You're just at the starting gate, you have to pick your battles wisely," he said. "Your career of public service will be short if you take on the whole world in your first week."

"Can't do that, Dad. I didn't enlist for this—I can't turn a blind eye to an unlawful arrest."

We said our goodbyes briefly as I hung up the phone. I sat by the bed with my head in my hands for an hour and thought; about an earlier conversation the two of us had had about the State Police. He had been around law enforcement a fair number of years. He had worked with various law enforcement agencies, and he held that the New Jersey State Police were, in fact, the best. Since 1921, they had built a reputation of trustworthiness and honor.

On the other hand, we were also aware of what happened four years earlier, in 1998, when an ugly racial profiling controversy had emerged. Two troopers had shot and wounded two African American men and one Latino in a van on the New Jersey Turnpike. The van had been pulled over for speeding as its occupants were on their way to a basketball tryout in North Carolina. When the driver accidentally put the van in reverse, an officer, having pre-decided this was a drug bust, fired eleven shot into the interior.

Falsified reports had entered into that case, too. An investigation had found that racial-based targeting was widespread within the police culture. In the end, the federal government had become involved in monitoring the NJSP. I had known about these things, but made a decision to be the best representative of a state trooper I could be within these ranks.

Tired as I was, I slept no better than fitfully after I hit the pillow.

A matter of hours later, not altogether refreshed, I drove my car back to work for another day. Reporting to the Tuckerton State Police barracks, I greeted my fellow troopers and performed the daily tasks of taking out the day's trash, making coffee, and cleaning dirty dishes. New troopers are always expected to attend to these "housework" chores. I began to set up the patrol car with a shotgun, flashlight, and road flares.

It was nice to carry out these simple, non-controversial tasks as I deliberated on how to approach my issue with Trooper Cole. He certainly showed no sign of concern over the unlawful arrest. To hear him tell it, the previous shift seemed to be a good day's work. He had congratulated me and regaled his buddies with our exploits. Now he emerged from the barracks as I was preparing the car for service. Again he was all about business as usual, checking through my preparations and climbing into the car to get our patrol underway.

I let an hour pass before I found that I couldn't stand the tension—the "elephant in the room," as it was, at least, from my end. I swallowed hard and spoke: "Sir, with all due respect, what you did last night was wrong."

Trooper Cole turned and measured me with startled eyes. It was as if I had reached across the interior of the car and slapped him in the face.

"What did you say?"

"Arresting the women for drunk driving was wrong, sir. There was no probable cause, plain and simple." Did I want to say the following line? I said it: "And I won't testify in court to support that arrest."

Hours, days, years of silence seemed to follow—of course, that's only how it feels when the tension is thick. After a few moments, Cole slowed the car on the Garden State Parkway and turned slowly to face me. I noticed the calm was gone, replaced by a reddening complexion. "Who do you think you are, Hopson?" he demanded. He glared at me for a second before adding, in a more ominous tone, "You'd better keep your mouth shut. Besides, what makes a 'boot' like you an expert on probable cause?"

I made no attempt to argue, but simply stuck to my position. I felt he could see that I meant business and would not be intimidated into covering up for him. Angry, he pressed the accelerator and our patrol rounds resumed, speaking to one another only when absolutely necessary.

In a bare moment, my world had changed forever. Looking back, that point in time, by the side of the road on the Garden State Parkway, was the end of my innocent youth and the beginning of adulthood. But my position on this incident was a matter of fact, and my announcement of it had gone about as well as could be expected. My relationship with my trainer was now on the rockiest ground possible.

There may have been scores of little things Cole might have taught me during the rest of that shift, but he kept his own counsel. Training was terminated, thus endeth the lesson. The difference from the previous evening, when he had been calm and fraternal while instructing me, made a stark contrast. And that was the state of my work life over the following ten weeks. I was *persona non grata,* disloyal and self-righteous in the eyes of my assigned trainer. If I was going to learn the daily skills I needed, I'd have to do it some other way. I began to teach myself the ropes as best I could.

It wasn't long before I received a subpoena to appear in court in reference to Krista's case, which still remained on the docket as a DUI arrest. Cole seemed to have no fears over what I might do or say, or perhaps he was calling my bluff. His impunity over that night's unlawful arrest spoke volumes about the state of things.

I began to think about what I could do to bring the truth to light in court. It wasn't as if my standing was unassailable: I had assisted in the arrest, helped issue the tickets, and participated in an untruthful report. This was a matter of confession as well as accusation. It seemed I was damned if I did, damned if I didn't. How could I have gotten myself into such a situation in only eleven days of duty?

I came to the conclusion that it wasn't all about me; I had taken my stance because the truth was the truth. It needed to be respected, regardless of the consequences.

The morning of the court hearing, I entered the judge's chambers to consult with the municipal court prosecutor. I wasn't surprised to see Cole waiting in chambers with a look of calm confidence. No matter what his demeanor suggested, he had to be wondering which way the wind was going to blow. Was I going to play along, as he had demanded? Or was I going to crash and burn by taking on his good name? He wasn't going to find out from me until the moment of truth arrived.

The prosecutor summoned us to his desk, peered up at me, and asked, "Hey, troop—I watched the videotape of the drunk driving car stop. Are you sure Krista was driving the car?"

I answered without delay in order to preempt Cole from controlling the narrative. "Sir, she was not driving the vehicle," I said simply. "She was in the backseat."

The prosecutor raised an eyebrow and turned to Trooper Cole. No one spoke for a moment; this wasn't exactly an everyday situation. The prosecutor wanted Cole to address the discrepancy, and finally the trooper nodded assent—what else could he do, given that the video was in evidence? However, he held firm on the obstruction charge. She had taken flight, even if she had done so during an illegal arrest. The prosecutor reluctantly granted his request and dropped the drunk driving charge and the traffic tickets. I felt vindicated to some extent.

Outside the judge's chambers I saw Krista and, for the first time, the driver from that fateful night. It turned out that he was her cousin rather than a stranger she had met at a party. On the night of the arrest, he'd been driving with a suspended license. She had protected his name out of family loyalty. Krista now pled guilty of obstruction—a violation, I learned, of an earlier probation she was serving.

Trooper Cole and some of his friends might have said that those facts bore out his identification of Krista as a "scum bag"—that she was already on probation, she was protecting a guy who was driving on a suspended license, and the two of them deserved whatever they got. I didn't see things that way. She was admittedly no angel, and I hope she's found her way to a more positive and law-abiding life. But she is a citizen, someone's daughter, and as deserving as anyone else of every basic right our Constitution guarantees.

I knew what my eyes had told me, and what the videotape confirmed. I knew how the law applied to both driver and passenger. Nothing could have been more clear-cut. For me, the only question was how the truth could prove so difficult to win through, particularly in the context of training for law enforcement.

I took a deep breath and slept a little better. I had prevailed in the first round. But the fight was far from over. As a matter of fact, it had hardly begun.

I might have been just another rookie. I might have been a face in the crowd, had things gone down differently; one more "boot" fixing the coffee and cleaning the restroom; another cog in the wheel.

It's difficult to avoid speculating. What if I'd been assigned to some other trainer, one who did things legally? What if I'd gotten a year or two into my career before being confronted with an unfair choice between "loyalty" and honesty? Maybe I'd have been on stronger footing among the troopers by that time. Maybe I would have known better ways of handling the Trooper Coles of the World.

None of that mattered now; it was what it was. When I publicly contradicted Trooper Cole's arrest report, I lost any chance of quietly establishing myself. Unbeknownst to me at the time, I had broken the "blue wall of silence" which insulates police from the public. Now everyone knew my name, particularly the older guys. Justin Hopson, it was said, could not be trusted. This Hopson was a "whistle-blower," a snitch. He was too high and mighty to be one of us.

The peer pressure I experienced is unique to the police world. Police have a certain way of getting things done. We size each other up and ultimately render the verdict: you're either *one of us* or you're not, and the difference constitutes a wide chasm.

The guy who is *one of us* is the one who can be trusted to play by the unwritten rules. If he crosses over into a gray area while following those rules, we are going to "have his back." Therefore he will have our backs when the time comes. The result is a considerable strength in numbers, and men find that it brings a secure sense of belonging and identity. But they absolutely will not tolerate rebellion. They will pay great prices to be included in that solidarity, prices that might be paid by their longstanding beliefs or values.

I would have enjoyed the fellowship and camaraderie of fitting in. I suppose what made me different was the premium I placed on my personal integrity and standards of conduct. It wasn't news to me that some law enforcement officers cut corners with the law. But I would not be stiff-armed into becoming one of those officers.

When I decided to apply for the New Jersey State Police, I intended to be a point of light, a good example for those who came behind me. And when I came to the fork in the road, that point where it was either go along or go alone—well, I had to make a hard-edged personal choice. Mine was to remain true to my ideals, which are legal, personal, and constitutionally based.

I didn't mind going it alone. The problem was that I wasn't going to be *left* alone. There's quite a difference, and I learned that quickly.

Part of the male system of belonging involves hazing, and it's a fairly universal practice. Rookies pay their informal dues in a variety of groups, and in a variety of ways. You'll find hazing in a college fraternity or military service academies. The newcomer must prove he is worthy by fighting his way through the door to full, unquestioned membership status—to settle the question once and for all that he has the right stuff to become "one of us." Accept the hazing today and you can dish it out tomorrow.

Not that "dishing it out tomorrow" was much of a motivator for me. I never cared much for lording anything over others. Yet I'd become accustomed to a military environment at the academy; I expected to pay some informal dues, and I had no complaints about the normal ones. However, it was becoming clear that my hazing would be a little more serious. Perhaps the goal wouldn't be to motivate me through the front door, but to maneuver me out the back one.

I had to watch my back, knowing that no one else would. In the beginning, my strategy was to keep a stiff upper lip and demonstrate that I was man enough to handle whatever the challenge may be. I wasn't going to complain or retaliate.

My hazing began to show a nastier streak. It was a few weeks after Krista's day in court, and I was reporting for duty at the barracks. As I walked through the locker room to change into my uniform, a senior trooper who stood six foot six and had the build of a linebacker collided into me - in a way that was clearly no accident on his part. The trooper, named Max Williamson growled, "Yo," and glared at me. I received the message, but chose to disregard it. That was my basic policy for this kind of thing.

As I attended to my locker, Max spoke again. "I'm talking to you!" he snapped. I turned back to face him. His stance made it clear what he wanted me to see: a tee shirt bearing the phrase *Lords of Discipline.*

Other than its ominous sound, I had no idea what the phrase signified. I would find out soon enough. The phrase was probably drawn from a best-selling novel by Pat Conroy, published in 1980 and filmed in 1983. Set in the early sixties, Conroy's novel is a highly fictionalized account of some of his own experiences as a military cadet at The Citadel, the Charleston, South Carolina military academy. In the novel, the narrator matches his wits against a secret organization called The Ten. These ten secret "lords of discipline," with the covert endorsement of the school administration, use terror tactics to rid the academy of undesirable candidates—in this case, the school's first African American cadet.

"The Ten" presumably came from the author's imagination rather than anything that really happened at The Citadel, and Conroy has said as much. But he didn't invent the principle of secretly organized enforcers doing an institution's dirty work behind the scenes. It's a fact of history and probably everyday life.

Conroy clearly wants us to be horrified by the idea of "lords of discipline," but apparently someone in the field of law enforcement found it to be a workable premise. And now the phrase was being used to put certain vivid ideas in my mind.

I wasn't spirited away in the night by white-robed enforcers, as happened in Conroy's tale. I suppose Trooper Max Williamson was letting me off with a warning, as patrol officers will occasionally do with those who are slightly speeding. The message was this: *You are on a very short leash, my friend. You had better watch your step.*

Chapter 3:

In the Name of the Lords

My life at the barracks became a bit tense. The trick was to focus on one day at a time—get through this shift, and don't think about next week. Don't question how long this treatment is going to continue.

The Chinese had a method of slow execution called the "death of a thousand cuts." The idea is that the little things add up, and the devil is in the details. So much of what I faced in this, the darkest period of my life, was trifling, even petty. But it took its ongoing toll.

If I entered the report room, where the other troopers would gather, one of two things might occur: The room would suddenly fall into silence, or it would empty as a number of troopers got up and left. It can be unnerving to know you're always being watched, particularly when it's with a high degree of contempt.

Then I would walk over to check my work mailbox, only to find it stuffed with stacks of blank transfer request forms. I could feel the snickering behind my back and couldn't help thinking, *Maybe they're right. Why not walk away and get a fresh start?*

The only two problems with that strategy were, one, that it wasn't in my character to surrender, and two, where could I go? It was a small state. My reputation would precede me and things would be no different at the next barracks. I removed the forms and tossed them onto the table, thinking, *Nice try—I'll make my own career decisions, thank you.*

It wasn't just what was in my mailbox, but what wasn't. Police reports and personal information were stolen from me. And there was the regular bruising collision with Max Williamson who had worn the Lords of Discipline tee shirt. I found myself keeping an eye out for him, feeling a sense of dread when I knew he was in the building.

One day, having finished my work shift, I was tired and ready to go home. I left the barracks, walked to my car, and found a disgusting brown substance coating the driver's side of my car. It was chewing tobacco, spat from the mouth of one of my "fans." Another time I found an insulting cartoon glued to the windshield of my car.

I thought maybe the incidents would fade away with time, and that the troopers would find some other target for their unwanted attentions. But I lived in a state of constant dread for months. After a while, persecution has a certain effect. No matter how much you believe in the rightness of your cause, no matter how logical and ethical you feel about your stance, you still begin to think, *What's wrong with me? Why do they hate me so much? Why can't they understand that I simply want to be honest and by-the-book?*

I did have the foresight to keep a good record of everything that happened. I considered a threatening or derogatory note to be evidence, and I preserved it carefully. When I was shoved or was at the receiving end of some other mistreatment, I wrote down the time, place, and details. The time would come when I'd be thankful I'd taken the pains to do this.

In July of 2002, I reported for duty and found a note taped to my locker at eye level. Even though typed and formally addressed to

"Trooper Hopson," there was nothing official about the correspondence. It was an abusive, threatening note, specifying the probable cause position that differed from my training officer. "Lose the chip on your shoulder," it read, "Or someone will take care of it for you." The note concluded, "If you believe that everyone is warm and fuzzy, and if you're not prepared to deal with someone who may wish to harm you and others, then maybe you should join the Peace Corps." In other words, the people I wanted to protect and serve were the enemy, and respecting their rights was being "warm and fuzzy." The State Police had no place for such idealism as obeying the U.S. Constitution. Their "right" was wrong in my eyes, and my right was wrong in theirs. And they wanted me to know that I was a marked man.

I then took the lock in my hand and attempted to push the key into it, but it wouldn't advance. Chewing gum had been forced into the keyhole.

As I walked into the report room, it was clear that everyone knew what gifts had awaited me. The men were eager to see my reaction. I asked to speak to my sergeant, who was visibly amused, suppressing a fit of the giggles. "I'd like to speak to you about the note on my locker," I said.

"I'm not aware of any notes," he smirked.

My mailbox was in the report room, and now I turned to find a note posted to it, too. It turned out to be identical to the one posted on my locker.

I had to admit that these guys had covered the bases. I now knew just how serious my opponents were taking this situation, and just how juvenile they were capable of being. Steaming on the inside while trying not to show it on the outside, I went on patrol.

It was Trooper Cole himself who approached me on the following day. As I was getting dressed for patrol, he called my name and asked to speak with me in the detective's office.

When I got there, I felt as if I was reporting to the high school principal for detention. Cole was sitting behind a desk, and the arrangement was for me sit before him like an unruly ninth grader. When I arrived, he looked up at me and said, "You just don't get it, do you, bud?"

I answered in as neutral language as I could muster; I would not be baited. Cole went into a tirade what kind of "boot" would question his training officer, where he got off contradicting him on probable cause, and so on. None of this was new, but eventually he came around to the real agenda: He did *not* want this winding road to lead to an internal affairs investigation. He was talking tough, but it was clear that he was beginning to feel a little uncomfortable himself. I was glad to know I wasn't alone.

Trooper Cole reminded me that this whole thing came down to Krista who was, in fact, a "scumbag" with a prior record. To his mind, that was key legal point.

I restated my position, in all its simplicity. Arresting Krista was not justifiable. There is no probable cause for arresting a visible non-driver for drunken driving. I was unwilling to violate the law in the pursuit of an arrest statistic.

So much for the defense; now I went on the offense. "As long as we're here, Trooper Cole, I want to talk about those notes on my locker and my mailbox," I said. "There was also gum stuck into my lock. Who is trying to intimidate me? Where do you stand on that kind of thing?"

"I don't know what to tell you," Trooper Cole shrugged. "I have no idea who did that stuff." He didn't seem overly concerned, but it was clear that the meeting was over. We parted without much cordiality.

The intimidation continued as usual. I was bumped and shoved regularly, I received more notes ridiculing and insulting me; other troopers looked through me as if I were not in the room, or they left the room as soon as I entered it. I was the outcast of the barracks. I couldn't leave anything of value on the premises, because vandalism was always a strong possibility.

There was a far more troubling issue. Irritating as harassment at the barracks could be, there hadn't been any true danger. Going out on patrol, however, opened up other possibilities. Did I really know who could be trusted and who couldn't? In a situation requiring me to call for backup, I had to consider the possibility that I wouldn't receive the support I needed. This, of course, affected my decision-making.

I began to wonder if I could take this critical issue to those in authority. Still a rookie and without rank yet; it was better to resolve a problem personally when possible. But I was beginning to see that there might be no other option.

One day at the State Police barracks, I recognized a sergeant I knew, and wondered if this may be my opening. He was in the process of washing his car. I wanted to be careful about how I raised the issue, so that I could gauge his response before putting all my cards on the table. "Sir," I said, "I have some questions I'd like to ask you about hazing."

I told him a little about what was happening to me on a regular basis. I tried not to approach the subject as whining or complaining, but as a young boot wanting to know what he could logically expect.

The sergeant listened quietly before turning off the hose and facing me. "No, Trooper Hopson," he said, "hazing of that degree is not typical at all, and you shouldn't be having to deal with it." He turned back to his car, began wiping it down, and forgot I was there. His answer had been rather vague and non-committal. Still, I hoped he would grow interested in my predicament and investigate it himself, and maybe step in to mediate. As far as I know, however, he never made that move.

It was September of 2002 when I reported for duty one day to find that menacing Max Williamson was present and seated in the report room. Whenever he was around, I knew that a body slam would be somewhere on the day's agenda.

As I checked my mailbox, I saw that his eyes were boring into me with laser intensity. Nor did he let up. Max was going to stare at me until I responded in some way. I tried to simply ignore him and walk in the direction of my seat, which happened to lie in the opposite direction. This only caused him to rise from his chair and follow my steps. From my peripheral vision, I saw Max place his left hand on his hip, with elbow thrust outward. *There it is,* I thought, *attack formation. Here we go again.*

Or not. *No,* I suddenly decided. I wasn't going to cooperate this time. As we passed one another, I tightened my upper body at the critical moment. His elbow jab bounced away, a misfire. When I looked over my shoulder a moment later, I saw his surprise and anger.

It was right off the playgrounds of elementary school. That was my daily life during much of 2002.

Sometimes, when things are going badly, all you can hope for is a change in the culture. If the mayor of a town is ineffective, you hope a new mayor will change things. If the sheriff looks the other way and lets the guys in the black hats shoot up Main Street, you daydream about a "new sheriff in town," someone who will take out the garbage. Fresh eyes are more likely to see a problem for what it is, rather than accept it as the status quo. Given my situation, I was determined to wait my adversaries out; sooner or later someone would come along, recognize a bad situation, and help me set it right.

A new sergeant named Calvin Cooper, walked into our barracks one day. I had no idea where he stood on the issue of illegal arrest, but I was about to find out. Sergeant Cooper happened to be standing nearby and saw me opening yet another derogatory note, demanding that I transfer elsewhere or find a new line of work. I wasn't happy for him to be seeing this—how could he know who was in the right? Maybe I was a sorry excuse for a trooper, and I was being rightfully chastised.

I saw the new sergeant watching me, and our eyes met. Something in his demeanor told me he was genuinely concerned, potentially sympathetic. I walked up to Sergeant Cooper and said, "Sir, I wonder if I might speak to you privately." He assented and walked me to an adjacent room.

It had been six months, and I discovered that I was more than ready to unburden myself. The whole story came tumbling out, from Krista's arrest, to the day in court, to all the episodes of harassment. I told how my car and my locker had been vandalized, how I had been pushed and shoved, how I had received threatening notes, and particularly how I was working without the assurance of being safe when I called for backup.

Sergeant Cooper listened quietly, shook his head sadly, and then shook my hand with firm reassurance. For the first time, I felt that I had an ally—someone with the power to help me out.

I went about my daily patrol for a few hours and unexpectedly received a radio message to come off duty and report to the barracks. I was instructed to come to the detective's office to meet with Sergeant Cooper and Lieutenant Symanski, the station commander of the Tuckerton State Police Barracks. "Tell the lieutenant what you've told me," said Cooper.

I had prepared myself for this moment. I brought copies of the threatening notes I'd received. I read entries from my written log, documenting the hazing and harassment in careful detail. All the names, places, and methods were there.

Meanwhile, I watched carefully to see the lieutenant's reaction. He was clearly uncomfortable with what he was hearing. I saw the beads of sweat accumulating on his wrinkled brow. He was finding himself in a tough spot, given that he had allowed these things to go on for some time. Now, however, he claimed to be appalled. "This is harassment," he declared. "Trooper Hopson, I want you to know that I plan to contact the right people and have these allegations thoroughly investigated."

My demeanor was calm and unemotional throughout. I said, "Lieutenant, I'm not looking for an internal affairs situation. And I have absolutely no desire to get anyone in trouble. All I'm asking is for the hazing to stop."

But Symanski had to worry about saving face at this point. He was one of the good ole boys associated with the Lords of Discipline. So he needed to distance himself from systematic persecution. "Well, I have to notify internal affairs," he said. "This thing has just gone too far." Yet interestingly, Lieutenant Symanski wanted to know why I had kept a journal.

"Sir, I think that anyone in his right mind would do the same thing," I replied. "If people treat you in inappropriate ways, it's your duty to keep a record of them."

"I understand. Anything further?"

I said, "Yes sir. My concern at this point is what might happen if I come forward with these allegations. I'm talking about the ramifications it might have on my career."

Symanski sighed deeply and replied, "I'm worried too, Hopson."

Thus began an immediate barrage of paperwork, phone calls, and the experience of watching everyone read a memorandum from headquarters about discrimination, harassment, and hostile work environments. With great ceremony, it was assured that everyone got the memo. But I knew it was all a bit of a charade. Headquarters clearly had no desire to address the issue head-on, therefore it simply tossed out a sheet of paper saying, "Don't treat people badly." Nothing was likely to change.

On the other hand, I was "growing up" quickly; fear has that effect. The longer the hazing continued, the more clues I picked up about the forces behind it. I was able to isolate a few specific troopers who clearly gave the marching orders. And I was able to discern that these were all affiliated with the mysterious group known as the "Lords of Discipline."

I wondered if the history books would shed any light on my situation. I began to find out all that I could about the New Jersey State Police, with the objective of learning whatever facts were known about the Lords of Discipline.

It's not the kind of thing you can look up in the World Book Encyclopedia. I spent time in the newspaper archives, among the few written books, and on the Internet. I talked to veteran troopers who were willing to talk. The information was elusive, but it began to materialize.

The Lords of Discipline (LOD), I discovered, have been operating just below the public radar since the 1980s. I came across a book called *Troopers Behind the Badge*, written by John Stark, who freely discusses hazing within the ranks of the State Police. "Nobody knows how or when it happens," he writes. "But the Phantom keeps everyone in line." [1]

I found it revealing that the author would feel comfortable about documenting such a thing. It appears that this kind of harassment, or "keeping everyone in line," in his euphemism, has been an accepted part of life for two decades among New Jersey's finest. As a matter of fact, it was the New Jersey State Police Memorial Association that published Stark's book in 1993. How, I wondered, has this practice gone so long without being challenged?

The Lords have turned up in newspapers. Fellow state troopers have casually observed the LOD for years. Just within the edge of

1   John Stark, *Troopers Behind the Badge* (NJSPMA, Inc. 1993), p.26.

the shadows, they've gone about their quiet but persuasive work of enforcing standards that may or may not be legal. And yet, to this very day, the official policy of the Attorney General of New Jersey is that there is no such group of troopers known as the Lords of Discipline.

What kinds of issues have prompted their action? From what I could discover, troopers have been targeted when they complained about racial discrimination, or racial profiling of the kind that occurred in the 1998 case I've already mentioned. More recently they've come down upon those troopers who dare to publicly criticize the State Police, and upon those like myself who have dared to report improper or illegal behavior at the hands of state troopers. The guiding lights of the Lords are conformity and protecting the status quo, whatever that may be. The weapons are fear and intimidation.

I had to promise confidentiality to some veterans, but I heard stories of death threats, physical assaults, and emotional punishment. I learned how the Lords had broken into and thrown lockers onto parking lots. As a matter of fact, my own case demonstrated how the Lords were preoccupied with lockers. Lockers and mailboxes are a trooper's visible symbols in the barracks when he isn't there. If you can't quite get away with battering the individual, you can do things to his locker. I heard about one that was vandalized and cleverly rigged in such a fashion that when the trooper tried to open it, he slashed his hand so severely that it ended his career. Another footprint of reign was the list of rules and regulations that was posted and signed by the LOD on the lockers of newly appointed troopers.

The Lords might also vandalize cars or any other personal possessions. Nails were used to hammer home intimidation. They had been known to drive nails into the car tires and work boots of targeted troopers. Rumor campaigns have served as a devastating weapon as well; one of the best ways to intimidate someone is to damage his good name. Unfair Poor performance reviews have been another method of souring a law enforcement career.

My friend was a rookie trooper in the 1990's. After returning from a summer vacation, he learned that his uniforms were thrown in a shower. His uniform sleeves were tied together with salt placed in the pockets. The Lords poured salt on his gear on three occasions to intimidate him. Why salt? Saltiness is a strong taste that is distinctive; it is the opposite of blandness. In the New Jersey State Police, you are not allowed to be "salty"; you had better not "stand out" from the group, but fall into line. After we talked about his experience, the only advice I could offer my friend was to stay clear of me and find a good dry cleaner.

We can say this about the Lords: by hiding behind secrecy and covert acts of vandalism, they establish themselves as cowards. I was willing to stand behind what I had done, but not a single Lord would come forward to do the same thing. How many men like Max Williamson have been associated with this group over twenty years, as the "Lords" or the "Phantom"? I would guess they'd number in the hundreds.

But let it also be said that a select few have spoken out against them. Some of them have been women. Some have been African Americans, or of Hispanic origins. Some of them were simply guys like me who happened to believe in the code of ethics. They've compared the Lords of Discipline to the Ku Klux Klan and other hazing organizations. Some members of the State Police, often victims themselves, have come forward to denounce something that should never exist amongst those who wear the badge to protect us in a free society. All the while, the powers that be have chosen to look the other way, to claim there is no such culture, and to feign astonishment when publicly confronted with actions they've known about all along.

I personally spoke with those few and heard their counsel when the opportunity presented itself. I had to consider the depth of my willingness to keep on with this thing. Was I biting off more than I could chew? I wondered, *what if they do something more violent than colliding into me or throwing my locker in the street? What exactly am I going to accomplish by continuing to butt my head against this strong, twenty-year-old wall? Do I have a martyr's complex or what?*

No, I didn't have any kind of complex. At least I didn't think that was the case. What I did have was one heck of a stubborn streak. I believed that the law and my integrity were two things worth fighting for; now was my time to fight. I was not going to give in to these people. I would see it through.

Chapter 4:

The Strange Legacy of John Oliva

Summer heat gave way to cooler weather. I hoped that somehow my life would cool down a bit, too. Yet events quickly took another unpredictable turn. On the first day of October, I got the news about John Oliva.

They found him outside a church in Absecon, New Jersey. At the age of thirty-six, the state trooper had taken his own life, his body discovered by a churchgoer. The body was lying in the autumn grass, face to the sky. Beside it were a .40-caliber Glock handgun, a photograph of the trooper's girlfriend, and a few other personal items.

The State Police issued a press release lamenting the tragic loss of one of its own. The trooper, said the report, had been on "administrative leave." It wasn't long, however, before I began to fill in the blanks and learn the whole sordid tale.

Like me, Oliva had been speaking out about corruption on the force. In the newspapers and in court, he was raising serious questions about the New Jersey State Police. Therefore he had attracted the same anger and retaliation that I had. The administrative leave was, in fact, a leave of absence to deal with emotional stress, brought on by the hazing. Oliva was deeply depressed, in psychiatric consultation, and taking prescription medication for severe anxiety.

In October, however, he had been due to return to active duty. Rather than go back to whatever treatment he was expecting, the trooper decided to end his life. So he gathered a few precious treasures, walked to a church near his home, and discharged his Glock into his chest.

I was deeply troubled when I heard the news. Not only did I wonder what terrible forces could lurk behind such a tragedy—I also began to wonder what it might mean to my own situation.

I decided to learn all that I could about the strange life and death of Trooper Oliva. The more I read, the more tragic I found his story to be. John Oliva was a former football star, a martial arts expert, a marine, a municipal police officer, and finally a state trooper who graduated *first* in his academy class in 1998. Here was the last man who seemed likely to take his own life; an achiever; a go-getter, as evidenced by his diverse accomplishments. He was the most likely to succeed, the least likely to be driven to such an unthinkable end.

Oliva told one newspaper that even with all the options before him, including his success as a municipal cop, it had always been his special dream to be a state trooper. Reading that statement sent an uncomfortable chill of recognition down my spine.

The tipping point between his promising ascent and his tragic decline occurred in his indoctrination with the New Jersey State Police. In May of 2001, as I was preparing to begin my career in law enforcement, John Oliva was filing suit against the State Police in federal court. He claimed he was being systematically trained to single out suspects on a racial basis. When he refused to play that game, he began to suffer the consequences.

It had all started when he was, like me, a fresh-faced boot just out of the academy. This was the very time when racial profiling among our troopers was surfacing as a systemic problem. The 1998

New Jersey Turnpike case, with eleven shots being fired into a van, occurred only two months after Oliva's graduation from the academy. It was splashed across *The New York Times*, it was the subject of inquiries and disputes, and it was the talk of the locker room at every barracks in the Garden State.

Oliva had clashed with his trainer. It turned out that he was not okay with arresting people illegally, particularly on a casual, daily basis. Again, I thought: *same song, different verse.*

Oliva's training officer would drive the patrol car to the I-76 ramp at Camden. He would park in a grassy area where Oliva would be told to keep an eye out for certain racial types. The idea was to pull them over, find the drugs, then write the ticket and figure out the probable cause later. It could all be whitewashed in the paperwork.

During his first two training weeks, Oliva and his supervisor wrote four traffic tickets for "failure to maintain lane." Oliva later testified that in each case, the charges were—for lack of a better term—lies. "We never even followed them," he said. "We made up the violation to justify the stops."

When Oliva complained, the Lords of Discipline quickly stepped up and made their presence known. Oliva's gear was vandalized, the usual threatening notes were stuffed in his mailbox, and discrediting rumors were spread about him.

Eventually Oliva had turned to Internal Affairs for help, but he was shocked to find the accusations turned back against him. Headquarters suggested that he himself was the problem and a willing participant in racial profiling. This was a man who had excelled everywhere from the football field to the Marine Corps to city police, but now his life was one round of discipline after another, both official and unofficial. Meanwhile, his trainer was actually *promoted*, even as Oliva's serious charges against him were on the record. Remarkably, Oliva's trainer became an instructor at the academy and in 2001 taught me police tactics.

Oliva's suit was filed in April 2001, and the "discipline" intensified. Oliva struggled to cope with all the obstacles being thrown into his path. Before long he was forced to take stress leave. He began antidepressant medication to calm his nerves, regularly visited a psychologist and a psychiatrist, and gradually gave up hope. When the time came to return to active service, he chose instead to end his life at a church in his neighborhood. No one was certain whether he had ever worshiped there. I can only speculate that, in his despair, a house of God must have seemed to him a symbol of both earthly peace and eternal justice.

As the media picked up Oliva's story, my own problems were suddenly one giant step closer to the light of public awareness. I hadn't known it, but Oliva and I had been occupying parallel hells, though his had begun four years earlier. How should his tragic end affect my own problem? Was I doomed to repeat his sad history? Or was it now more critical than ever that I stand up and be heard?

If I quit now, maybe John Oliva's charges would be filed away and forgotten, then he would have died in vain, and I would live the rest of my life with that realization. Maybe, just maybe, his tragedy could be part of some redemptive solution, a public mandate to clean up the New Jersey State Police.

Newspaper reports linked John Oliva's troubles with the Lords of Discipline. They had gotten the better of Oliva. How could I keep them from prevailing over me?

After some reflection, I decided to attend Trooper Oliva's viewing at the funeral home. I found that I had a deep desire to pay my respects to his family, to somehow show them the connection I felt to the one they had loved and lost. I just didn't particularly want to be overly discreet in my attendance. Therefore I dressed in civilian attire and tried to slip in quietly.

It wasn't a very comfortable experience. Some part of me wondered if this could be a preview of coming attractions. But it felt like the right thing to do, being there to honor John and support his family.

In the reception line, I noticed a very emotional husband and wife ahead of me. The husband caught my eye and asked if I'd been one of John's friends. "No sir," I said. "I'm sorry to say we never met."

The husband began to explain that he knew John Oliva from the local fitness club. He had never known anyone so healthy, so fit, so disciplined. "How could this happen?" he asked, shaking his head with bewilderment. "It just doesn't make any sense." I could only nod quietly and sympathize.

Over in a corner of the room there was a makeshift shrine of pictures paying homage to John Oliva's life, so short on time and long on accomplishments. Again I marveled at what a fine person, what a valuable civic leader, had been systematically destroyed to such horrible purpose—being found guilty of integrity by a jury of his peers.

Then, in the open coffin, I finally saw John himself. Again there were pictures and mementos by his side—things that were important to him. I looked hard at his face, wondering what secrets lay behind those tranquil features. What advice would he give me if he could open his eyes and speak at this moment? His weeping family stood all around, including John, Sr., the father. My heart went out to the plight of parents outliving a child of whom they were so clearly bursting with pride, and now better understood my own father's stance.

I shook the hand of John Oliva, Sr. Though I was a stranger and not emotionally demonstrative, I pulled him to a near embrace. "Sir, I am a fellow trooper," I began. "I never had the privilege of meeting your son." I waited for eye contact before adding, "What I want you to know is that he did *not* die in vain. Your son's sacrifice will change the New Jersey State Police. And the so-called Lords of Discipline will be dealt with. I wanted you to be sure about that."

He found it hard to speak, but a dawning awareness appeared in his wet eyes. "You're like John, aren't you?" he asked simply.

Those words sent a chill down my spine. I just looked back at him.

"You *are*," he said, more confidently. "You're like him."

I was increasingly aware of those behind me, waiting patiently to express their condolences. But Mr. Oliva wouldn't let me go quite yet. His energy seemed to be coming back as he seized my shoulder and said flatly, "I want five badge numbers."

I nodded slowly. He went on, "It took four years, but they broke my son. They *broke* him." Grief was giving way to rage. Mr. Oliva brought his wife and daughter to his side and made introductions all around. He told me his address and invited me to come by his home for a visit. I promised I'd do so and solemnly left the scene.

Even at this moment, I wondered, who knows I'm here? Who is watching?

Eights months into my career, other than more hazing, I had waited so long while nothing happened. The Oliva tragedy turned everything upside down. It wasn't difficult to see what was happening. My standoff was teetering on the edge of public notice by now. A few days ago I'd been little more than a troublesome gnat to brush away. Not anymore. With one public relations nightmare in the paper, the revelation of a similar one would constitute a pattern. Instead of a gnat, the department would be dealing with a hornet's nest.

Only one day after my visit to the funeral home, Lieutenant Symanski called me at home. He dispensed with small talk rather quickly, cleared his throat, and gave me the news.

"Hopson, we're processing a transfer order on you as we speak," he said. "They're shipping you to the Bordentown State Police barracks. Central part of the state—effective immediately."

It had come so suddenly that I found it difficult to wrap my mind around the news. I asked, "Sir, is this fairly ordinary—this kind of transfer?"

"Not at all," he replied in a hollow tone. "Actually I've never seen a transfer handled like this."

I could tell that his political position had suddenly shifted in an unhappy direction, and I frankly didn't feel a great amount of sympathy. For nearly a year, he had sat back and watched the show. Only the entrance of a new sergeant and the Oliva tragedy had put my harassment on the front burner. Best of all were these words: *effective immediately.* I would have my bags packed and be gone by the time the news got to the Tuckerton barracks water cooler. They would have absolutely no time to throw a bon voyage party, and I would receive no farewell body slam by menacing Max Williamson.

What this really meant was that the powers that be knew they'd better handle the case with kid gloves. My evidence of hazing added up to a powder keg waiting to go off. Given the media attention, it seemed likely that Internal Affairs was becoming much more interested. I was now asked to meet with them in a highly confidential setting, in which I would provide a formal statement about my allegations of hazing and my description of an organization known as the Lords of Discipline.

I was none too enthusiastic about an Internal Affairs inquiry - not my idea of a helpful career move. Given my discomfort about going on the record on this scale, I asked my father to attend as both counsel and witness. With his years of experience and prominence in the field, he would be an invaluable asset. He knew both sides—law enforcement bureaucracy and his son—intimately. I also knew I would be reassured by his presence.

When the two of us arrived at the discrete offices of Internal Affairs Bureau (IAB), we were greeted by an eager group of detectives.

It was obvious that they were ready to sink their teeth into this case, and they wanted to hear every single detail I could tell them. If this was a dubious professional move for me, it was precisely the opposite for these detectives. I was their ticket to headlines and job promotions. Internal Affairs was historically all about rooting out corruption, and they could be both invaluable or a bull in china shop. Sometimes the IAB was a great force for cleaning up the system; other times, it was more interested in grandstanding and playing politics.

It's not that I'm impossible to please, but I wanted to avoid the extremes. I didn't want to be secretly hazed by the LOD, nor did I want to be publicly exploited by the IAB.

One way or another, I was ready to resolve this matter once and for all and get on with my life. The best-case scenario was for me to share all the facts and hope that the system would work— that the detectives would pass on their information properly. Then the hierarchy would make appropriate changes so that hazing was eliminated from the New Jersey State Police. It required some powerful optimism to see things going quite that neatly.

In any case, I gave them everything I had: chronology, notes, names, background. What it came down to was that I had refused to support an unlawful arrest and was hazed by a secretive group of troopers known as the Lords of Discipline. Could I prove they existed? Well, I had seen LOD tee shirts, read a list of rules and regulations posted and signed by the LOD, and interviewed others victimized by the group. I certainly wasn't the first trooper to ever announce the group's cult-like existence.

The detectives wrote it all down. They were delighted with my detailed recordkeeping. For hours, they squeezed every fact and every observation from me. These same facts had been greeted with indifference back at the barracks; now they were embraced as if each sentence were a bombshell. I was so grateful for my father's presence. Just as I'd anticipated, he was the perfect buffer between my reticence and the detectives' zeal. I knew he was looking out for my best interests, and the IAB representatives knew that he understood how they worked.

At the end of the meeting, one of the lead detectives said, "Trooper Hopson, we want to express our appreciation to you for having the courage to come forward like this. As you well know, we had to get you out of Tuckerton for your personal safety. Now we're determined to conduct a thorough investigation, and we believe you've given us all the ammunition we need."

"I don't need to be thanked—it's a matter of doing my duty," I said. "But sir, I have the same concerns I've had all along. First, I still have to think about my personal safety, even well up the road from Tuckerton. Second, I have to think about my career. It's still my life goal to be a law enforcement officer in my home state. I'm not sure how freely I can pursue my career once I've been labeled as a whistle-blower on police misconduct. I just want you to understand that I've put everything on the line here in order to cooperate with your investigation. I know you're determined to see that some of these things are cleaned up—but how can I be sure you'll watch out for my own personal well-being?"

The detectives layered on the generic reassurance. I had done the right thing, they said, and they pledged that I had nothing to be worried about, that I would be fully protected. The specifics of how they would do that—well, details were not forthcoming.

Chapter 5:

Changes in Latitudes, Changes in Attitudes

I was excited and a little apprehensive about reporting to a new barracks. This represented a fresh start, but I understood that, realistically, there could be no such thing as a true "do-over." The world of the New Jersey State Police is a small circle, and word travels quickly—by telephone, teletype, and tell-a-trooper. Everyone knew what was going on, and whistle-blowers aren't readily embraced. I know one trooper who later described my greeting as that of a leper among the healthy.

Getting established here would be an uphill battle, but I wasn't asking for the moon. I just wanted to come to work without being hazed or singled out. I didn't mind working to earn new friendships. I figure I can make friends eventually wherever I go, regardless of the circumstances. Here I was under the microscope and I knew it, but I was glad to be relocated and ready to work.

Meanwhile I was surprised to find myself dating again. I met an attractive young lady, and we seemed to like each other. I was doing well just to manage work relationships; it was hard to see how a nervous wreck like myself could be much of a romantic prize right now. Then again, relationships tend to bloom when we least expect them. And I had a deep need for a little caring in my life.

At a restaurant, on our first date, we shared the usual basics. I could see the apprehension in her eyes when I told her my line of work. *Great,* I thought. *I've scared her off.* But we moved onto other topics, and we found it very easy to have an enjoyable conversation. I felt some of my tension melting away, and that felt really good; I hadn't realized just how much I needed to relax and be a normal guy in his late twenties even just for an evening. We continued to date, and the relationship was a kind of saving grace, a positive and nurturing gift during a tough period.

Then, with a pang of anxiety, I heard from Internal Affairs again. It was late October 2002, by this time. The detectives wanted another "highly confidential" interview. I wondered if I had opened the proverbial Pandora's box, though my father had known from the beginning it would be like this. Again, I asked him to come along for moral support and counsel. Again, the lead detective was eagerly waiting to whisk us into a private room to be interviewed. There was a desk, a tape recorder, a television, a VCR, and a box of facial tissue. As we were seated, the detective told us the biggest news. "Trooper Hopson, we've now investigated all your allegations from the first meeting," he said. "Each one of them has been verified."

I said that it came as no surprise to me.

"We studied the videotape of the drunk driving arrest," he continued. "Then we followed up by interviewing the occupants of the red sedan. Just as you said, it was a white male driving. It's also clear that everyone knew it, including your trainer. The blonde-headed girl was charged even though she was in the back seat. The driver ran because he had no license. As a matter of fact, Trooper Hopson, they told us that they all ran at first, when the car pulled into the trailer park. The men kept going, but the women panicked and returned to the vehicle."

"It makes sense," I nodded.

"Key moment on the video," said the detective, "was the voice of Trooper Cole saying these words: 'The guy driving the car ditched.' So it's obvious that the truth was on your side, and that your trainer—by his own self-incriminating words—made an unlawful arrest, lied about it, and allowed you to be hazed. The whole thing is frankly sickening. It's sickening for your sake, for the sake of those arrested, and for all of us who depend on law and justice."

There wasn't much I could say in response to these things. But now the detective pulled his chair a few inches closer. He said, "These facts will be presented to the top administration of the New Jersey State Police. And those people will recognize your courage and integrity just as we did." Somehow, I felt both vindication and a new round of tension.

The writing was now on the wall. As my father and I left the bureau, I released a heavy sigh and told him, "Thank God for videotape."

There was nothing to do but get on with my life and work. I continued to accustom myself to Bordentown and its environs, and to work at building relationships with the troopers there.

One day I drove to the barracks with my mind on the details of a court hearing for a criminal case. As I walked through the door, however, I was told to report to the office of the Sergeant First Class for what he identified as "bad news." *Wonderful,* I thought, *what now?*

The sergeant filled me in. "Trooper, you need to be informed that you are now the target of a sensitive internal investigation."

I could only stammer, "What?"

He looked at his paperwork. "It's been initiated against you by Lieutenant Symanski from southern New Jersey, your old barracks."

Somewhere inside, I wasn't surprised at all. How could I be surprised by any new development in this unhappy narrative? "So what's going on here?" I asked.

"My suggestion is to exercise your right to remain silent," he said, "as in your Miranda rights, which I now have to read you."

"Wonderful."

He did exactly that, telling me that I had the right to an attorney, that anything I said could be held against me in court, and all the rest.

With a shaky hand, I then signed a Miranda card, proof that constitutional law had been duly observed. The sergeant shook his head slowly and said, "This is the first time I've ever had to do this with a trooper."

I repeated my question. "Sergeant, what is going on here? What exactly am I being charged with?"

He picked up the paperwork again and explained that I was being investigated for theft and falsification of reports relating to an address change and mileage reimbursement.

I said before that little could surprise me. This was an exception.

"Sir," I said with rising anger. "On the first day I reported for duty, I notified my senior sergeant at Tuckerton of my relocation to a new condo that I shared with another trooper—and he advised me not to worry about filling out the paperwork! For six months my relocation was inconsequential. But now he's turning me in for taking his advice."

"That so?"

"Yes sir. It's retaliation. I refused to support an illegal arrest, and I was hazed for it and interviewed by Internal Affairs about it. That's what this is really all about."

"Hey Hopson, whatever happened to your roommate?"

"Sir, we lost touch soon after the LOD investigation began."

"That so?"

The sergeant maintained his carefully objective stance. I'm sure it all struck him as another fine mess to stay out of. "I'm handling the situation according to standard operating procedure," he said, pushing the paperwork away and picking up his coffee. "You're dismissed," he said.

As I left the office, I knew the important thing was to control my rising frustration and anger. I turned to God, praying silently that he would protect me since it seemed as if I couldn't protect myself. The Bible says, "The truth shall set you free," and I believed that. But so far it had only entangled me in ever-deeper webs, the way we tell our children that a lie, not the truth, is supposed to do. I could only cling to what I knew was right, and hope the others were letting enough rope out to eventually hang themselves.

The question was this: *Why would Internal Affairs entertain these new allegations at all?* Were they playing both ends against the middle—and if so, why? Surely they could see what was going on with Tuckerton. They knew these trivial charges against me were part of a petty agenda of retaliation. Just a week after Symanski had been interviewed about my hazing, he had suddenly filed charges about mileage reimbursement and address changes. But IAB had duly processed his paperwork; they had refused to protect me or even give me a heads-up.

Eventually, Symanski's allegations were dismissed and I was cleared of all charges. But those accusations gave me one more thing to worry about when I least needed it.

The Christmas season of 2002 was a bit strange. The end of the year is a time to huddle with family, look back nostalgically on the blessings of another twelve months, and set resolutions for the coming twelve. Make no mistake about it: I had been through the strangest year of my life. Glad as I was to have it behind me, I had no rational assurance that 2003 held any real promise.

Other than my parents, none of my family or friends knew about these developments in my life. As I went to parties and gatherings, everyone wanted to know how I was enjoying being a part of New Jersey's finest. "I bet you could tell us some stories," they grinned.

"I'll bet I could, too," I replied with hidden irony. I just couldn't handle opening the can of worms that results from telling my loved ones about the Lords of Discipline. Again, I didn't want them to constantly worry and wasn't sure they would really believe the whole story, anyway. And even if they did, I didn't want them trying to push me into some other line of work. I love my family and my friends, but this was a road that I felt should be traveled light, with as little baggage as possible.

Also, I suppose it was in the back of my mind that this whole nightmare would just blow over at some point, somehow. I was out of sight, out of mind for the Tuckerton Lords, right? And didn't they have as much to lose, or even more, by pushing this grudge against me? Time can heal a lot of wounds, and I had put my trust in that, otherwise I wouldn't still be a trooper at this point. At least for this Christmas, I smiled, hoped for the best, and continued to play the local role of "our own Trooper Hopson."

I needed the brief interlude of rest, because January meant a new and hectic pace. During the day, I was performing all the duties of a state trooper, which alone is exhaustive. Meanwhile, I was taking phone calls from Internal Affairs, handling court cases, and seeing to due diligence regarding the hazing.

I was glad to be working, grateful to have "left the scene of the crime." But still there was the feeling that I was a team player on the wrong team. I tried to give one hundred percent to every task and responsibility, to be loyal and easy to work with—but the others still kept their distance. They weren't cruel and contemptuous like the troopers of Tuckerton, merely aloof. The administration was no better. I was an unpleasant reminder of everything that could go wrong in our line of work.

Whenever it all began to get me down, I thought about John Oliva and his family. In due time, I'd reintroduce myself and share my experience with the Oliva family. I still remembered the haunted look in John Sr.'s eyes when I promised them I would see that John didn't die in vain. Then I tried to think about all those troopers going through the academy this year, next year, and on into the future. Maybe what happened to me wouldn't have to happen to them.

So I soldiered on solo, went out on my daily patrols, came home, and took the phone calls from Internal Affairs. I gave them every speck of information I had on the Lords of Discipline, knowing that at some point the Lords could well decide they didn't want this Hopson character talking about them.

And I had very real grounds for worrying about that, because our case was leaked to the newspapers. State detectives had been going about their investigation at the Tuckerton barracks, and lo and behold, they discovered Lords of Discipline tee shirts in the lockers of troopers. It was another example of trooper arrogance, feeling that they could plaster their secret organization on a shirt without even needing to keep the shirts out of sight. Other troopers verified that they had seen these.

The tee shirts provided just the nugget the news media wanted— something tangible to wrap a story around. Now we'd come full circle. What had started with a quiet patrol, a trainer, his protégé, and a red sedan was now a statewide controversy.

IAB was able to prove that more than one hundred Lords of Discipline tee shirts were produced and sold. They were blue in color with profiles of the faces of New Jersey State Troopers on the front, and a list of LOD-affiliated barracks on the back.

In time, the official position of the superintendent and the Office of the Attorney General would be that these were "informal" shirts, kind of a locker room joke, if anything. They would point out that no other physical evidence existed. But what about the shirts with its list of official "franchises" of the Lords of Discipline or the list of rules and regulations which had been given to rookie troopers.

If, technically speaking, there was no more "physical" evidence; there was indeed the electronic variety. Computer hard drives yielded document files that turned out to be threatening messages and unofficial memos of the types I had received. These pointed directly to the Lords of Discipline.

Then there was testimony: the stories that had been told to me, and in particular one from the lips of a high-ranking state police official. In exchange for confidentiality, he testified about meetings held by troopers to suggest the specific names of troopers who needed the group's special brand of "discipline." In their view, hazing was to control those who "embarrassed the organization." To the astonishment of many of us, the official verified that State Police officials actually conducted these meetings.

Troopers such as Kim Zanilla, Ann Jones, Edwardo Garcia, Dan Stevenson, AJ Wilson, and Kirk Witherspoon provided consistent testimony that unearthed widespread hazing within the ranks of the State Police.

It was clear that my case was not an isolated incident. I had brought to light a problem that had spread out of control like a virus. A small handful of us, including John Oliva, had simply proven too stubborn to back down. But what next? The problem was out in the open; I was now the reluctant public symbol of resistance to a rogue cop element—one there would be public pressure, ironically enough, to discipline. What could I do other than continue to submit to interviews and cooperate with systemic trial and disclosure?

A rock had been overturned, and the ugly things beneath it had been exposed to the light. Even so, I wasn't certain that state bureaucracy would be willing to heal itself. There were probably those who felt that the Lords were an example of law enforcement's "sausage making"—the idea that we all enjoy sausage, but we wouldn't enjoy seeing exactly how it's made. Cynics would say that such messiness as the LOD is simply how police departments are "made." A police department has to keep everyone in line, and sometimes it has to cut a few corners to do so.

Some of us begged to differ.

As I thought of all this, I realized again that I was in way over my head. If this whole episode was too big for me, at least it wasn't too big for God. I regularly fell to my knees and prayed for his will to be done, for his presence in the long and troubling journey. I found comfort in the familiar words of Psalm 23: "He restoreth my soul: he leadeth me in the paths of righteousness for his name's sake. Yea, though I walk through the valley of the shadow of death, I will fear no evil: for thou art with me; thy rod and thy staff they comfort me . . . in the presence of mine enemies."

Now there was a new round of troubling phone calls. The State Police had developed an interest in my movements at certain times, and in certain places. Several state troopers, it seemed, had run my vehicle's license plate through a database. They were seeking access to personal information about me. The official who called to tell me about this was now following up; he wanted me to disclose my whereabouts on certain dates over a five-month period of time. He said that the State Police would be investigating the matter, and he was telling me all this in the interest of my safety.

"Who were the troopers?" I asked.

"These issues are currently being investigated," he replied in a cloud of legalese. "At present, we're unfortunately not at liberty to identify the troopers." In other words, they were at liberty to put a scare into me, but not to give me any information I could use for protection.

"Well, thanks for the heads-up," I said with a measure of sarcasm.

So people were accessing the facts and details of my life. I knew it wasn't for the purpose of surprising me with a bouquet of roses, so I had to watch my back both on and off duty. The official called back, this time to take a recorded statement from me. I expressed, loud and clear, that I had deep concerns for my safety. The official concluded the interview, then offered an off-the-record comment: "Don't take this the wrong way, Hopson, but I wouldn't want to be in your shoes." Actually, I didn't like being in them myself; but I took his meaning: *Be on guard, my friend.*

I now decided it was time to share my secret with a few friends and family members, to their understandable shock and concern. I legally secured a .357 magnum handgun and kept it at my bedside table in the house I recently bought. The two-story starter home was surrounded by mature trees and had lots of windows. But the windows seemed to shrill with every wind gust, which created sporadic noises throughout the night. Whenever I was home, I made regular checks on the doors and windows to be certain they were secure. I was constantly on edge, always listening and watching, and this kind of life will take its toll after a while. I knew I couldn't live like this forever. But I had no choice. The people I had to worry about may be New Jersey's finest, but they weren't necessarily New Jersey's smartest. One of them could make a spontaneous decision to come at me at any time.

I sat in my bedroom night after night, waiting out the darkness and hoping tomorrow would bring some light at the end of a dark tunnel. I reflected on this strange, lifelong dream of law enforcement. That was a younger, more idealistic Justin that was now hard for me to recognize. But even now, there was enough of the romantic in me to think, *it doesn't have to be this way. It's always possible to change the culture.*

I remembered saying that last sentence to an old-timer on the force. He laughed sarcastically and said, "Hopson, you're just a cog in the wheel."

I couldn't understand at the time how right he was. It's a big machine, and it wears down its parts. And yet it's a funny thing about cogs. All it takes is one stubborn one, one bad fit, to throw the wheel off-course and shut down the whole huge mechanism. I was that cog. There was nothing enjoyable about it, but I was resolute. I would not be part of a bad machine, and I felt it was time for some serious maintenance service on the inner workings.

John Oliva had started it, and I was going to see it through—for him, for his parents, for all of us. His tragic life was over, but I had inherited his legacy. Though we had never known each other, our life purposes were now intertwined. I could not afford to fail.

Chapter 6:

Blue Walls All Around

I t's strange how things work. You can go your whole life without being aware of a certain word, or a type of car. Then, after the word arises in conversation, or your friend introduces you to that type of car, it seems to be everywhere you look.

Something like that happened to me with police misconduct.

I had a romantic idea of law enforcement when I was growing up. I realize that all too clearly now. It was a combination of the good guys I saw on TV, and my own father's occupational adventures, which cast my perception of police. I had seen a movie or two featuring "police corruption," and I figured that kind of thing existed in New York or L.A., but it seemed awfully melodramatic. Surely police corruption didn't occur nationwide.

But now that my ears were open, now that I knew it existed, I began to see this same problem cropping up in other places. There was the Oliva situation, of course. That one hit very close to home for me. But cases of police corruption and internal misconduct began to appear before my eyes in the national news, or on the television, and finally in my own research.

For example, there was the situation in Oakland, three thousand miles to the west and one year earlier than the event that turned my life upside down.

Keith Batt was a college graduate, a twenty-three-year-old man with the lifelong dream of serving a police force. He was three weeks out of training when he found out how the "real" cops did things.

After graduating from the police academy at the top of his class, Batt received his badge and was assigned to the nightshift on the west side in Oakland, California. That part of town was known for drug dealing. Far too quickly, Batt found himself taking on The Riders. He had expected that confronting gangs would be part of his challenge—he just didn't expect the gangs to be made of policemen. The Riders were fellow officers.

For three weeks, Batt witnessed falsification of reports. He saw violations of civil rights, including beatings, harassment, and drug-planting, involving ten different victims—all of them African American men. And Batt's training officer was one of the offenders.

Batt's trainer told him not to be a "snitch." Another of The Riders, while showing him various methods of circumventing police procedure, would smile and ask, "Are you ready for the dark side?" He seemed to enjoy flouting the rules.

One particular event provides a typical example. Just before two in the morning on June 19, 2000, Kenneth Soriano, 19, was packing his things for a trip later in the day. His car had been stolen, and he'd asked the local police to come by so he could make a report.

Batt, accompanied by an older cop, came to the door, and Soriano's Rottweiler began barking loudly. Soriano, accompanied by his cousin, came outdoors and began talking to the police at the front gate. Finally the cousin suggested that everyone come inside. It didn't turn out to be a good idea.

The dog just wouldn't stop barking and straining at his leash. The senior officer told Soriano that he would shoot the animal if it didn't quiet down. That remark made Soriano angry, and the cop continued to provoke an argument. As the discussion escalated into a confrontation, the two police officers restrained Soriano by taking hold of his wrists. When he quickly pulled away, the officers called for backup.

It took about two minutes for the room to be swarmed by a group of Oakland cops, who quickly overcame Soriano. They punched him repeatedly in the ribs as the older cop placed a "sleeper" hold on the man who had originally placed the call to the police to ask for assistance.

Soriano stopped fighting and put his hands behind his back, hoping the pounding would stop. He claimed that the older cop slammed his head to the ground at this point, and in fact there was a bloody gash above his left eye afterward.

The man was handcuffed. Then, he said, his body was kicked at least three times by police officers before he was jerked to his feet. Soriano's mother was watching the whole thing in horror.

An officer stood behind Soriano and searched him, saying, "You ain't got nothing on you, bitch!" The cop then punched him in the ribs.

As the man sat in the police cruiser for nearly half an hour, he was told he was in big trouble. Then he was asked to sign an incomplete police report. Once the signature was there, anything could be filled out on the rest of the form.

The senior officer instructed Batt to falsify the report. He was told to write that Soriano had elbowed him, starting the fight. In fact, the officer took the time to write out a false scenario on a separate sheet of paper, and ordered Batt to copy it onto the official report. [2]

---

2   Jim Herron Zamora, "Fellow Cops Told Me to Lie Testifies Whistle Blower," at http://articles.sfgate.com/2002-09-19/bay-area/17563311_1_police-officer-clarence-chuck-mabanag-west-oakland

This was one of any number of incidents. Batt witnessed them, sometimes found himself in the middle of the action, and tried complaining at headquarters. He went up the chain to his superior officer and talked about the regulations and codes of ethics he'd been learning and swearing to follow only a few weeks earlier. The officer listened patiently, then told him to forget everything he'd learned at police academy.

What could Batt do? Nothing more than what I would do, several months later in New Jersey. He reported for duty, rode on patrol, and hoped that somehow things would get better. Batt simply tried to keep his nose clean. But there are limits, even for those of us at the bottom of the food chain. When Batt saw the way a fellow rookie was forced into the template of corruption—assuring one more generation of police misbehavior—he had to speak out.

Batt's training officer ordered another young guy, fresh out of the academy, to make a false report and arrest. He was told to claim he'd seen a teenage suspect discarding seventeen rocks of cocaine, and to make the arrest on that basis. He hadn't seen any such thing, but the training officer wanted an arrest made. The falsified report would wrong two different young men—officer and alleged offender—in ways that could resonate throughout their lives.

The rookie, to Batt's disappointment, did as he was told. So Batt blew the whistle. He made a full report on the incident, and then tendered his resignation. Later, he was actually able to demonstrate in court that he was pressured to resign. He ended up as an officer in another community.

The complaints were followed up, and the result was a huge police scandal. The chief of police, of course, claimed that The Riders, a group of four officers, represented the full extent of the corruption. This is the standard method of denial—sure, those men you caught are guilty, but they're certainly not part of a pattern; problem solved, everyone go back to what you were doing.

The Riders were put on paid leave and charged with assault, kidnapping, and filing false reports. One of them, the supervisor who had told Batt to forget his training, went into hiding, probably in Mexico. His nickname among his fellow police was "Choker." Each of the Riders, incidentally, had a nickname. Another was known as "St. Jude the Foot Doctor" because of his expertise in wielding a police baton. He would go for the feet with it, sometimes when suspects were already on the ground.

When a case against a cop hits the headlines, past cases involving the rogue cop are endangered. In Oakland, about ninety drug-related cases had to be thrown out. Any lawyer who knew his client had been arrested by one of the Riders would have a field day creating reasonable doubt in court. At the same time, more than seventy civil rights suits were filed.

The cost of all this to the city, according to a civil attorney, could be $125 million or more. Now you can understand how administrators are likely to defend their reluctance to go after police misconduct cases. "There are always going to be bad cops, just like bad lawyers, bad doctors, or bad bus drivers," they'll say. "But the worst of them make plenty of good arrests. Are you willing to open the doors of the jail and let dozens of drug dealers go free? Do you want your police fighting themselves—or let them keep combating the crime on your street? Do you want to pay the taxes that will fund a string of civil suits? And finally, next time you're a victim of crime on the city streets, are you going to make these fine ethical distinctions when he comes to rescue you from a dangerous felon?"

The three remaining Riders went to trial twice, in 2003 and then in 2005. Their two million dollar legal fees were paid in full by a combination of police unions.

The first trial lasted a full year, one of the longest in local history, and ended with the jury deadlocked over the majority of the charges against the officers (they were declared not guilty on a smaller number of charges). The judge declared a mistrial, and two years later, the same thing happened again. One problem was that the district attorney had to depend upon a slate of former drug dealers and felons for testimony. These, the folks most likely to witness police misbehavior, don't make the best witnesses.

As a result, the three defendants were in position to ask for full reinstatement and the right to return to the nightshift on their former turf. The community was less than happy to see them back. Neighborhood residents, who had watched the antics of the cops for some time, saw the two decisions as official endorsements of the abuses they saw every day.

One of these, fifty-year-old Anthony McMillan, tells of watching an officer brutalize someone he encountered on the street. McMillan dared to remind the officer that his duty was "to protect and serve."

The officer looked at him and replied, "Where do you see that written on my car?" [3]

Much closer to home, over in Atlantic City, there was the case of Michele Zanes. It would not come to litigation for several years, but the situation was already in progress during my period of struggle.

Michele Zanes was a police officer with a strong personal faith. The time came when she found her prayers becoming much more urgent. She was finding herself in dangerous situations on the streets, calling for backup and getting no response.

Why? Officer Zanes believed her fellow cops were freezing her out because she was speaking out against her ongoing sexual harassment.

In a career often associated with the opposite gender, women need great courage to wear the police badge. They find themselves

---

3   Associated Press, "Oakland Struggles with Police Scandal," at http://www.
     berkeleydailyplanet.com/issue/2000-11-30/article/2415?headline=Oakland-
     struggles-with-police-scandal

surrounded by a fraternity of tough guys who follow an unspoken code to constantly re-demonstrate the "macho" way.

She was very patient. The harassment occurred over a period of six and a half years, and Zanes identified twenty-three officers who engaged in the misbehavior.

One day, as she was practicing at the police shooting range, a sergeant came up behind her and pushed his body up against hers, thrusting his genitals forward several times. That sergeant left her a handwritten note reading "Let me hold you tight, if only for one night!"

On another occasion, an officer gyrated his hips toward her in a suggestive fashion and asked, "Do you want some of this?"

Michele Zanes felt disgusted and humiliated, but she was like the rest of us—she wanted this job. These were unpleasant events, but they were rapidly over with. So why not just ignore them? Isn't that what we teach our children? When the other kids taunt you, try to resolve the situation without getting into a fight or resorting to tattling. Just ignore them, because that kind of individual is usually looking for attention, just trying to get a rise out of you. Don't give them that satisfaction.

That's what she did, and at times, she thought things were getting better. But Officer Zanes, too, had her limit, her breaking point. When a group of officers threw a dozen condoms on her Bible, she decided it was time to stand up and be heard.

She met with the usual rolling of eyes and advice to "grow a thicker skin." The attitude was that, after all, boys will be boys. But when she began naming names, life became dangerous. Sexual advances gave way to hostility. Then, when her life was on the line—silence. "Several times," she told a local TV station, "dispatch has asked if anybody was clear to back me up, and nobody responded on the air."

The pattern was clear enough. If you won't play ball with us in the locker room, we won't play ball with you on the street.

As her story became public during a sexual harassment lawsuit, it came to light that this was nothing out of the ordinary for the Atlantic City Police Department. From 1998 to the present, five women had been paid a total of $3.5 million in sexual harassment settlements.

One had testified that the sergeant suggested rubbing mayonnaise on her leg to resemble a male bodily fluid. Another woman was commonly called "cunt" by the other officers, and had regularly had pornography placed in her locker.

The settlements were paid, yet it never seemed to occur to anyone to address the situations making them necessary. Investigative reporter Jim Osman found that the guilty parties were rarely disciplined. In fact, many of them received generous promotions.

When Osman attempted to interview the sergeant about the mayonnaise comment, he said, "I wish you would take your ambush interview somewhere else." [4]

Something didn't connect. The police academies were teaching honor, ethics, and personal discipline. The instructors were doing everything they could to instill pride. Fine young men and women were graduating, getting their badges pinned, and taking their place on the blue wall, where they always expected to stand and protect our society.

But they quickly encountered another wall—a blue wall, in which police turned their backs on the public and faced inward, protecting only each other. Some of the instructors themselves were the most flagrantly guilty. Protect and serve? "Where do you see that written on my car?" said the officer in Oakland.

Some ingenious cops had a solution for this disconnection. Why not go ahead and start the hazing in the academy itself? Then the rookies could be disabused of their idealism before they went into the field.

---

4   Jim Osman, "I-Team: Badge of Shame," at http://cbs3.com/investigations/I. Team.Badge.2.291774.html

That's apparently what happened in New Braintree, Massachusetts. In late 2005, an investigation was launched into hazing at the agency's academy. Training procedures and practices were closely reviewed. The Boston Herald reported on the development, though a cloak of secrecy seemed to prevent many details from getting out, however, a few items surfaced. For example, there was a report that recruits' heads were being pushed into dirty toilets. Once again, a female trooper made the complaint.

There had been problems in the past. In 1988, a recruit died after collapsing during training exercises at the academy in Agawam. Fifteen other cadets were hospitalized with kidney ailments or symptoms of exhaustion. Yet in these cases, the Massachusetts attorney general held that state anti-hazing laws didn't apply to the police academy. [5]

The hits just kept on coming. In just a few cases, officers had been pushed to the point of speaking out, filing suit, or going to the press. The intimidation, the pressure groups, and the lawlessness were proved over and over. The only thing in doubt was the will of the governing bodies to make changes.

In a way, it was comforting to know that I was part of a determined group coming forward, and not alone against the world. Misery loves company, right? Perhaps I could reach out to other officers and troopers who had been through my situation, and who could help me get through the storm.

What a disillusioning revelation. Yes, I knew that everyone wasn't corrupt. There were plenty of great men and women in blue who were honorable, and I had already met my share of them. But what if they continued to be driven out by that other element, that element proving so resistant to change, even when it cost the department in so many ways—in money, in reputation, even in the backlog of arrests?

---

5   Associated Press, "Investigation Launched After Hazing Allegations at Police Academy," at http://www.neilrogers.com/news/articles/2005091618.html

At those prices, it couldn't be a coincidence that the wheels of bureaucracy were stuck when it came to reform. When budgets are being cut, yet a department pays out $3.5 million dollars to a series of plaintiffs, all because of ignorant, boorish behavior that could so easily be avoided—groping, offensive expletives, pornography in lockers—then we must be talking about an entrenched system. This must be a problem with roots so deep, they can't be pulled out unless a great number of strong individuals grab hold together and start yanking.

I could think of more pleasant things to do with my life, but I knew now that I was going to have to be one of those people. I increased my grip and resolved that I wouldn't let go.

Chapter 7:

Calling All Detectives

We are more dependent upon the kindness and encouragement of others than we ever realize.

In a given day, most of us get up and head for our places of work. Think about it. We might receive a goodbye kiss from a spouse, hugs from our children, smiles and greetings from colleagues, and maybe a few friendly texts or phone calls from good friends. Most of us have some kind of circle of support, whether we realize it or not. As the poet John Donne said, no man is an island. We are blessed by little interconnections to other lives. Sometimes we have their back, sometimes they have ours.

These support systems are like the gasoline in our cars. We don't tend to regard them much until they run dry. We only think we're driving along, but it's the fuel that's propelling us.

I learned this lesson well as time moved on. I was a single man whose divorced parents lived in other cities. I had few friends in the community; the plan had been for my life to be built around my work and my fellow officers. Everyone knows that men and women in areas of service—military, law enforcement, firefighters, or otherwise—develop tight bonds. I figured I would grow close to the other guys from the hours we'd spend together in patrol cars, in the barracks, or in the locker room. I would have friends who sustained me and whom I, in turn, helped to sustain.

Once I refused to buckle under, of course, it didn't work out that way. I was an outcast, and never had I felt more alone. When I did something right, there was no one to tell about it, no one to celebrate with. If I had a joke, who wanted to hear it? If there was some concern I needed to get off my chest, where was my confidante? I could only call my parents so many times. I needed friends through the rigors of the day. Now I had been transferred, and at least I could have a fresh start. My new patrol area was comprised of three small towns that dotted along two interstate highways. But I was a stranger in town nonetheless.

I had to hold a lot of things inside—questions, fears, emotions. I found myself losing sleep and battling headaches. There were bouts with anxiety and depression.

On workdays, at least I could stay busy, even if I felt my isolation acutely. It was simply a matter of focus—doing my job right and leaving no room for criticism; I knew no one was likely to cut me any slack, nor did I want them to; I wanted my work to be beyond reproach. On my days off, the inactivity took its toll. I admit to feeling sorry for myself, and having days when I wondered why I should even get out of bed.

I had yet to understand the reality of depression. We can't fight the enemy we don't recognize, and I simply failed to comprehend the depth of what was emotionally happening in my life. In the past, when I had gotten down or discouraged, I would just pick myself up. Like a lot of men, I believed it was that simple—that we just need to take responsibility for how we feel. Get busy, push on, and then we'll feel better. I had done that through the death of a loved one, or the breakup of a romantic relationship. I needed to realize that I was now in uncharted waters, at least in my experience. These emotions were on a different level of troubled.

It was something like being in a long, dark tunnel with no ray of light at the other end. Maybe there was no way out—how did I know? I had banked everything on this dream career I had chosen. I was a disciplined, focused individual who knew exactly what he wanted to do. Well, I had done it, and the dream had become a nightmare. What do you do when there is no Plan B?

I may have been down, but I still had my pride. If there was one thing I could control, it was this: I would not let my colleagues see how I was feeling. Many of them knew what had happened at my last post, and they were ready to see me falter. There was no way I was going to give them that satisfaction.

It meant there was an "elephant in the room" much of the time I was on duty. They knew the situation and I knew it—but I pretended everything was normal, and I didn't give a clue how I felt about the other troopers or anything else. I just did my job with a stiff upper lip.

And then something happened. I found out that I hadn't been wrong about the kind of career I was made for. The work was my salvation; there were days when I could find so much satisfaction in serving my community that I almost—*almost*—forgot about the situation that had ensnared me.

One day, for example, I was called to a local gasoline station where an armed robbery had just transpired. An attendant there had been held at gunpoint, and forced to hand over all the cash that was on hand. I felt the adrenaline rush of facing a real challenge, having an opportunity to use my training. This was the reason I'd enlisted.

I worked with other police departments in the vicinity, exchanging information in pursuit of leads for the robbery. I conducted a series of interviews, and later I was able to generate a photographic lineup of possible suspects. While this was going on, my life had a purpose. I was all about solving the crime, identifying the thief, and bringing him to justice. I guess all that nervous energy inside me had a healthy outlet.

Sometimes, unfortunately, the evidence doesn't add up to an arrest. We weren't able to close the case or recover the stolen money. Even so, it was a rewarding experience. For one thing, I learned. Classroom training is excellent, but the real world is the ultimate classroom. At the same time, I needed a powerful reminder of why I had gotten into this field. With all that was going on, I craved some kind of indication that I hadn't made a terrible decision. The process of investigation, with all its points and procedures, gave me that—as well as one big bonus. I had the opportunity to meet State Police Detective Everson.

He was the lead detective at my new barracks, and he came to me days after the armed robbery, asking to see me in his office. I knew who he was, of course, but I'd only had limited contact with him up to this moment. What I had observed was that this was a driven criminal investigator. He was fiercely dedicated to doing his job and finding the guilty.

That's why I was so surprised by what I heard as I approached his door: gales of laughter. Apparently he was on a phone call. I was a little nervous anyway, and I figured I could find better timing for barging in. So I waited a few minutes, amused to find out this hardnosed crime-fighter had a comic side to him. I had an idea I was going to like him.

He invited me in with a smile after I lightly tapped on his door. And he broke the ice quickly: "Hey, I don't believe everything I hear!"

"Sir?" I asked, taken a bit off guard.

"That's right, troop," said Everson. "I don't believe everything I hear." Seeing I was at a loss, he filled in the blanks. "Some of your buddies from Tuckerton seemed to want me to keep my distance from you. They say you're not to be trusted."

I sighed. "Yes, sir. I'm not surprised."

"Rumor has it you're a left-leaning liberal and an FBI plant, and you're out to take down the State Police. That right?"

"Well, sir, I—"

Everson quickly held up a hand. "I'm not interested in talking about your past, troop. I called you in to commend you for a job well done in the armed robbery investigation." He pushed a form toward me to sign—the standard commendation.

It was the last thing I expected; I must have looked at it as if it were a thousand-dollar bill.

"Um . . . thank you sir," I managed. I'd never received a commendation and by no means knew what one felt like.

I signed the form and looked up at the amused detective. "This means a lot to me, sir," I said. "Thank you."

The humor drained a bit from his face. "If you ever need to talk," he said softly, "I'll listen."

I nodded and excused myself from his office.

Back at my desk, I thanked God for a ray of hope.

There it was—a show of support, a personal connection. It's incredible the difference that is made by one gesture of encouragement.

I began to relax around Detective Everson. In time, I even began to open up and confide with him about the Lords of Discipline. I knew the other side of the story had gotten to him first, though thankfully, he'd taken it with a grain of salt. I wondered if he would greet my version with the same skepticism. He listened intently and assured me that he believed everything I told him. That meant a lot; it felt as if just a bit of the heavy weight on my shoulders was shifting elsewhere. There was someone in my daily life to help me know I wasn't alone.

Meanwhile, Everson began to teach me some of his craft. Having a mentor was another blessing, because I was hungry to take in every piece of information he was willing to share. Within a short period of time, I was studying the full gamut of criminal investigations from within the bureau. The detective arranged for me to be temporarily taken off uniformed road duty and placed in plainclothes as his assistant.

He must have realized what that meant in my life. Road duty hadn't been good to me so far. This was a way of moving in a new, fresh direction while staying with the New Jersey State Police. It placed me in a setting where I had a chance to thrive. I was working with a no-nonsense, work-driven encourager, and spending less time with those more likely to pick up where the Tuckerton boys had left off.

All things considered, even as I knew there were more challenges waiting ahead as the investigation moved on, it was really a best-case scenario.

I had the opportunity to work with agencies such as the Pennsylvania State Police, NecroSearch, the National Center for Missing and Exploited Children, and New Jersey's Department of Environmental Protection.

A key opportunity came when I was assigned a sexual assault case. Everson and I interviewed several witnesses, and worked toward the solution of a disturbing case involving a teenage boy and a forty-year-old woman named Debra. This woman, separated from her husband, lived with a son, nine, and a daughter, sixteen. If there's such a thing as an "ordinary" sexual assault case, this wasn't it.

The household was in shocking disarray. Debra had been allowing minors to engage in sexual activity and use recreational drugs. She'd had sex with a teenage boy in the family bathroom, in full view of her children. My heart went out to the children who had to spend their tender years in such a home. It made my blood boil.

Debra didn't seem particularly troubled by either her behavior or the fact she was caught in the act. I interviewed the apathetic mother, who had thinning hair and a weight problem that kept her from standing on her feet for any prolonged period. I began asking her about the goings-on in her home, and she finally began to fidget when one of my questions used the word *inappropriate*.

"What do you mean 'inappropriate'?" she asked.

I spelled it out for her: "Would you say your children saw anything they shouldn't have?"

She was a little off her game now, beginning to fidget. "They saw me with a boy, having sex in the bathroom," she admitted, quickly adding, "But that's only because the bathroom's got no door."

I looked at her and simply said, with a bit of unhidden irony, "Okay . . ."

"Well, I admit it was wrong, I'm sorry," she said dismissively. "But listen, we all have our needs, you know what I mean?"

The more we talked, the more Debra's skeletons came tumbling out of the closet. During a two-year period, she had presided over several house parties involving teenagers, alcohol, and sex. Debra had engaged in sexual intercourse with her daughter's seventeen-year-old boyfriend in the backseat of her car—illegally, a case of sexual assault (statutory rape). The same boy, meanwhile, had impregnated Debra's daughter. It was quite a challenge for me to contain my disgust.

My jaw nearly dropped when we got to the punch line: This woman made her living working around young people; she was the lunch lady at the local high school.

We arrested Debra, and she made all these confessions on tape. But then, of course, she was released on bail and back home with her children. Detective Everson and I got the Division of Youth and Family Services (DYFS) involved. We clued in the school district, too, and Debra was quickly suspended. Eventually she pled guilty in court and lost custody of her son.

I hoped that we had handled things well, for everyone concerned. I hoped Debra could somehow get her life under control, while being kept away from young people. Most of all, I hoped we had made a life-changing difference for those two children. Everyone deserves a better, more loving start than they'd been given.

It would have been nice to continue losing myself in my work, and perhaps create a brand new future after the awful beginning I had experienced. But I had set a chain of events in motions, and in February of 2003 the next domino fell.

Associated Press was reporting that the New Jersey Attorney General's Office had opened a multi-agency investigation into the Lords of Discipline. Newspapers gave brief details about a secret society of rogue troopers who "allegedly" hazed fellow officers. Peter Harvey, Attorney General at the time, offered the tough words that the public demands: "There will be no tolerance for the hazing or harassing of any trooper at any level not to mention New Jersey's citizens."

He would not "allow the deeds of a few to tarnish the reputation of many." Perhaps the most important information in the newspapers was an observation that this wasn't the first promise about dealing with the Lords.

So the probe was moving forward. As a matter of fact, there was substantial reason to think that perhaps there would be more than words this time. Internal Affairs informed me that tangible evidence had already been uncovered, leading to future suspensions for three troopers. I wanted to know what exactly had been uncovered, but the detectives wouldn't offer any details. They also reminded me that I wasn't permitted to discuss these matters with anyone else. That seemed to be the part they were most interested in.

I told them about my anxiety over the possibility of retaliation, especially now that news was coming out. The detectives coolly assured me they would relay my concerns to the proper authorities. Each time I talked with them, I came away with an increasing impression that my best interests weren't their top priority. Frankly, my impression was that they saw this as their moment in the sun; headline cases could become career moves. The Internal Affairs guys wanted to hit all the right notes, demonstrate a successful investigation, and win the prize promotions that such things always brought—all while neatly, politically, avoiding the rocking of any boats in state law enforcement.

It was easy to see that news of the Lords of Discipline was no revelation to these detectives. The hazing had gone on since long before their time, a kind of "open secret" that everyone knew and no one confronted. Now, of course, the press had turned up, and Internal Affairs had to demonstrate appropriate disapproval and credible action—but what about me? Where did my safety and future figure into the equation?

These things set me thinking again. As the song says, "Hello, darkness, my old friend." Things had been going well, but I could feel the positive vibes beginning to wear off as the inner whispers of self-recrimination returned. *You've done this, you know—you have no one to blame but yourself for what's about to happen to your career.*

I reached out for a medical solution, contacting our family doctor and friend. At his office, I gave him a condensed version of what was happening in my life, and my worries that things would only get worse before they got better. The doctor prescribed an antidepressant, carefully explaining the side effects.

I didn't resign my emotions entirely to a pill, however. I sought counseling, so that I could find healthy and proactive strategies for facing my fear and anxiety. There had been a time when I couldn't have imagined myself "going to a shrink." That was for crazy people, right? I now understood that it was for folks like myself who needed a little guidance in finding emotional clarity.

It was helpful that my counselor had worked with troopers in the past. He listened carefully to my story, as I shed a few tears in describing my struggles. But I was watching his reactions as closely as he was watching mine, and I saw that he was hearing a story that wasn't new to him. He knew these things happened, and he lauded my willingness to come forward and resist the corruption I had experienced.

"Because of you, the state can't run away from the problem anymore," he said. "At least I hope not. I've counseled a few troopers who have been victimized by the Lords of Discipline, and they were terrified of the idea of standing up to the abuse."

He sighed before continuing, "You've got a lot of courage and idealism, Justin, and I admire that in you. But I have to warn you all the same. I know how these men work, and I know how the system works. Fighting bureaucracy can be even more dangerous than fighting a few bullies. Keep your wits about you."

By the time I left that third session, I was more intense than ever. I realized I was bringing away more stress than I had taken in with me. Maybe I needed a different counselor.

More likely, I thought wryly, I needed a different life.

One day I would work a twelve-hour shift investigating crime. The next day I would go to counseling for anxiety. Life couldn't go on like this forever, and I knew that. But for the time being, I was going to be the good soldier and fight on, confronting one day's battles at a time.

Several times I received a call from the Deputy Attorney General (DAG), wanting to meet and discuss my allegations. During one work shift, I reported for a meeting with her at the state capitol. I remember pulling up to the Hughes Justice Complex, mentally rehearsing all the things I needed to remember to avoid worsening my plight during the interview. I climbed out of my patrol car, adjusting the visor forward on my hat, to cover my eyes.

I had to walk past two fellow troopers who were guarding the building. Little things like that couldn't be taken for granted now.

I nodded in a friendly way as we passed, and they nodded back. I signed the visitor log, stepped into a vacant elevator, and stood at the back of the car, feeling the tension that was stiffening my whole body. I realized my brow was perspiring more than it should be. My breaths felt tight and labored, but I took a couple of deep ones anyway. *Calm down,* I told myself. *You're not the one who should be afraid.*

The DAG looked a little too pleased to see me, considering the subject at hand. She motioned me to a chair, and we exchanged informalities. Quickly we turned to business, and she explained that I would have to testify in a general court martial against a State Police lieutenant, a sergeant, and a veteran trooper. But the idea was to handle everything administratively—neatly and discretely, really. "We have to look at the bigger picture here," she said. "We all want to do the right thing, but I know you would never want to be a part of anything ugly enough to hurt recruitment."

My eyes went dull. I sat back and sighed. This was an old enough argument, an appeal to my loyalty. "Patriotism," Samuel Johnson observed, "is the last refuge of a scoundrel."

In a flat tone, I repeated, *"Recruitment."*

With that, I rose from my chair and headed for the door. The shocked Deputy Attorney General called after me, "Trooper Hopson!"

But I kept walking. I had come here to the state capitol—the highest local authority in New Jersey. But it wasn't high enough; the blue wall loomed tall enough to overshadow even the Hughes Justice Complex. Even here, I was being told to play nice with lawbreakers; that civil rights violations and corrupt "law enforcement" were bad, but that the unpleasantness of dealing with them was worse. I still wasn't buying that.

The next morning, my father and I met with a former State Police superintendent at a local diner. He had spoken to my academy recruit class a year earlier, but this was the first occasion I'd had the privilege to meet him. I could remember him, his voice soft and serious, exhorting our class not to let a fifteen-minute car stop ruin a twenty-year career.

After a brief introduction over a cup of coffee, the superintendent looked at me and said, "You're a victim." Then he turned to my father and said, "We need more troopers like your son."

I was encouraged by his support. He offered to make some phone calls, but I smiled and politely declined. I had learned what I was up against. The short interview at the Hughes Justice Complex a day before, had shown me that we were in much deeper than what a few phone calls could remedy. We were up against a high and formidable blue wall.

I just hoped we were doing more than butting our heads against it.

Chapter 8:

Truth and Consequences

I spent months looking toward, and dreading, the general court-martial. As a matter of fact, I had the word of Internal Affairs that I wouldn't be placed in the position of testifying against my fellow troopers. Despite that promise, I had learned that my well-being was the priority of no one but myself, and that I should be ready for any eventuality.

Sure enough, on an early morning in August of 2003, I found myself driving to court to testify against Lieutenant Symanski, as well as Trooper Max Williamson and a veteran sergeant. These were the ringleaders of the Lords of Discipline at the Tuckerton State Police Barracks, and they faced charges related to hazing and their involvement in the Lords.

I came to the courthouse in Quakerbridge, just north of Trenton, and waited in the courthouse lobby. I was a little surprised not to be briefed by the prosecuting attorney, nor sequestered. This seemed like an important and controversial case—one that had been well covered in the media—yet there seemed to be a "business as usual" approach taken by the prosecutors. I sat in the lobby with the defendants against whom I'd be testifying, and they certainly made their presence known. They glared in my direction with the unbroken stares of boxers before a prizefight. As I began to grit my teeth on the broken promises of Internal Affairs, Deputy Attorney General Al Foramo finally arrived and whisked by my chair. He instructed me to stay put until I was called to testify. It wasn't exactly a comfortable or calming situation.

I tried to sit and focus on my task, my words, and the simple adherence to truth that had brought me to this point. I didn't look in the direction of those doing the staring, but I reviewed the key events in my mind—the unlawful arrest, the falsified report, and the pressures of intimidation the Lords of Discipline had unleashed.

Finally we were called into court. As the court-martial began, Lieutenant Symanski and the co-defending Trooper Max Williamson were asked for their pleas on the multiple charges; these two had apparently received some real-world advice from their attorneys, and they were ready to cut their losses. They pled guilty and were immediately suspended without pay.

But there was also the sergeant, a man I had long suspected to be a key leader among the Lords of Discipline. He stood in defiance, pleading not guilty to the pending charges against him.

The trial now began. I was summoned to testify by the presiding judge, and I attempted to approach the stand with confidence. At all times, I had reminded myself that I had truth and integrity on my side. The Bible tells us, "You will know the truth, and the truth will set you free." I may not have felt any freedom then, but I had to believe that I would in time.

I hoped my demeanor and confident stride masked the anxiety I felt when I took the stand and swore to the oath. The first sight I took in was the defendant. He looked absolutely carefree—a man in absolutely no fear of the law or its findings. I wondered if he had private reasons to be so sure of himself.

Deputy Attorney General Al Foramo began his line of questioning with the March 2002 car stop and the arrest of Krista. With smooth narrative, skill, he led me through the important events of that evening, underlining the shocking breaches of procedure and integrity.

My focus was keeping my testimony clear and articulate. Predictably enough, the defense attorney objected several times in an attempt to throw me off rhythm and cast doubt on my story or my objectivity. Usually, the judge overruled him and ordered me to proceed. But when we got to the matter of the inaccurate police report, the objection was loud and adamant. As a matter of fact, when I testified to participating in a criminal act, the defense attorney immediately demanded a mistrial due to my exposure. The insistent defense attorney advised that I be read my Miranda rights.

The maneuver had no chance of succeeding. He simply wanted to highlight my involvement in the wrongs I'd reported. Again, the defense attorney needed any possible opportunity for making me seem untrustworthy or hypocritical.

I was a little worried, and it turned out that I wasn't the only one. The court recessed to consider this claim. During the break, I approached Deputy Attorney General Foramo and asked him what the heck was going on. The two of us stepped outside the courthouse, and Foramo pulled out his phone and began making calls. I couldn't help but notice his concern, his incessant pacing, and the fact that he'd begun sweating profusely. Foramo disconnected from one of his calls and told me I needed a special letter establishing immunity, so that I wouldn't be held liable for the false report. It would have been very nice if someone had thought of this before the trial was in process.

After a few tense moments of speaking with the Attorney General, Foramo provided the court with a declamation of immunity on my behalf. Foramo already had the necessary immunity letter in his possession but, in an oversight, failed to locate it amongst his court documents. I recall thinking, *this guy isn't prepared for trial.*

Within the hour the court-martial was in progress once again, and I continued my account. I had to face cross-examination from the aggressive defense attorney, of course. His strategy was to hammer away at the accuracy of specific dates in my written chronology, trying to show me to be confused or unreliable. It wasn't much of a battle plan. Throughout my testimony, I gave plain and consistent answers to the questions, and, if I didn't recall some detail, I said so.

I think the defense attorney realized the law of diminishing returns would set in at some point. I wasn't going to fall apart, I wasn't going to prove unreliable, and I wasn't going to do anything but weaken the defendant's case if I remained on the stand. So I was finally asked to step down and exit the courtroom.

It was hard to believe I'd gotten through it. None of my fears had materialized; there was no reason they should have, as I always knew the facts, and they were straightforward. Still, a courtroom is an intimidating place, and you always know the lawyer sitting on the other side is trying to paint you in an unfavorable light, whatever the facts may be.

Ultimately, when the system works, there is really no legal defense against the truth—*when* it works. It did on this occasion. The once carefree and fearless sergeant was found guilty on multiple counts and later suspended without pay. When I heard of the outcome, I wondered what expression the sergeant cast when the judge handed down the verdict.

So now it was all out there. I had stepped forward, blown the proverbial whistle, and put my story on the record under oath. As it turned out, I was the keynote speaker of the court-martial calling out fellow officers. Maybe there would be a few people out there, readers of newspapers, who would quickly peruse the story over their morning coffee and observe the truths brought forward by a young officer. They would approve. Then they would turn to the sports page, and within a few hours my name would be forgotten.

New Jersey State Troopers, however, would not be likely to forget. I knew they would follow the story a little more closely. Friends of the three officers would be resentful; others might see me in a new light, an uncomfortable one. I could only hope a few of them would get the message that it was okay to stand up, to come forward, and to speak out.

In any case, it was time to find out how my career would proceed. I would take it on with the same attitude I'd brought to the witness stand: outer confidence no matter what I felt inside; simple honesty and attention to the facts; humility and courtesy.

Suddenly I could look at my life in a more relaxed way, as most people do. The court date had hung around my neck like an albatross, and now I felt free to actually live. I had been dating the same young lady all the while, and she figured into some of my plans. She had helped me through the anxious months. She'd been a source of strength and nurturing at a time when I needed it. I really felt God had brought her along at a time of tremendous need.

I had a few friends, and of course there was my family. All of them seemed to have the same advice: Get out of here! Go to the ocean, the mountains, somewhere you can wear a Hawaiian shirt rather than trooper blue; somewhere as far away as possible. It didn't take much thought to figure out where that should be. Why not Hawaii itself? My mother lived there. So I made arrangements for a trip that would accomplish two goals: visiting Mom and "fleeing the scene of the crime." I would take my girlfriend, and neither of us would speak of or even think about work.

Ten days in the most beautiful setting on earth is definitely good for mind, body, and spirit. There's certainly nothing in New Jersey like the sunshine, tropical flowers, and exotic fruit that abound in Hawaii. We visited local surf shops and ate at offbeat cafés. The people delighted us—easygoing, friendly, and fun.

It also felt good to see my mother for the first time in too long. While my father had been the closer parent geographically, my mom had played an essential role in my life, and we were very close. She had always listened, nurtured my hopes, and supported my dreams. My parents had divorced when I was two, so I had grown up without knowing what it was like to be with both of them under one roof. I've spent my life wishing that had been different, but we take life as it comes to us, and whatever the situation may be, there is something of wisdom and practicality to come from it. Sometimes it's the things we don't have that go the furthest to make us what we are. I've come to understand that the essentials of family life are truth and forgiveness, and I learned about them from my mother.

I sat with my mother and shared the entire saga of my inauspicious beginning as a state trooper. She listened in astonishment, sadness, and shock, and then smiled and said, "I'm so proud of you, Justin." It felt good when she wrapped her arms around my shoulders and said, "You're going to win, because you're standing on the truth."

She just seemed to understand me. That's how it is with mothers. I knew this was a trip I was supposed to take, a time of sanctuary and rejuvenation so many thousands of miles away from my troubles. Here, on the sunny beach with my girlfriend, New Jersey seemed to be something from another lifetime. Its cold highways couldn't reach across the wide sea to touch me.

Ten days is a short time, and I had to go back. But when I did, I was rested and strong, ready for another round. My temporary plainclothes assignment had ended so it was time to suit up in uniform again. I was actually looking forward to donning the hat with the badge and hitting the highways and byways once again.

It was all business as I got back to my patrol duty. Several cases were awaiting my attention. As I looked them over, I realized there were skills that needed development on my part. I began to think about attending a specialized school and getting some fresh training. I was thinking of these things, focused on the future, as I dressed in uniform again and left for patrol—my first shift back at work. Within minutes, the newly appointed station commander summoned me back to the barracks. "What now?" I wondered. I turned the car around headed back the way I had come.

I walked into the lieutenant's office with, I'm sure, a question on my face. He promptly handed me a memo notifying me that I was to appear before a re-enlistment board in two weeks. Frankly I wasn't clear on the purpose of this.

"Sir?" I asked. "Can you tell me why I would need to be at a re-enlistment board?"

He had a poker face. Busy shuffling other papers, he said, "Issues have been brought to light that the board will need to address." He was well schooled in bureaucratic non-speak.

"What issues?" I persisted.

He looked up, considered his word choices, and said, "Possible job-related issues." When pressed, he at least provided me with a worst-case scenario: I wouldn't be re-enlisted as a member of the State Police.

I stood for a minute and let that sink in. I had my Hawaii tan, my new, mellower attitude, and a tank full of fresh energy. I was ready to serve my community. But the Lords, or more accurately, those who stood behind them, were not going to let go of me.

I said, "Fired?"

The lieutenant was hard to read. He now gave me some good advice, suggesting I call the State Police union and ask for assistance. Then he reminded me that I needed to sign the notification form. As I applied my signature, I felt like I was putting my name to a resignation. They were going to try and fire me. Where did it end?

As I left the barracks, I thought about what to do. I decided that the person I needed to consult first was my academy class instructor. From my observation, she had an excellent grasp of this type of situation. I gave her a call, and, not surprisingly, my story had gotten there first. She knew all about what I'd been through, and she thoroughly approved of the stance I had taken. But there wasn't anything she could specifically to do intervene from her position.

My next move was to contact State Police headquarters and see what I could find out. Naturally, I was greeted by careful, bureaucratic language. All they knew was that it would be a good idea to get an attorney.

What was next? If there was no help from the academy or from HQ itself, maybe I needed to talk to people who actually cared about me personally. I called a friend and fellow trooper and told him that I was facing an interview with the re-enlistment board, my job on the line. He thought about my predicament and suggested I register with the Whistleblower Protection Program, and, of course—hire an attorney. The Whistleblower Protection Act is a federal law passed in 1989. It protects any government employee reporting misconduct. It comes into effect when an agency threatens to take some form of action against an employee who reports misconduct of some kind. This was a course of action that made sense for me, but I knew it involved further legal entanglement. For me, the idea was to make life increasingly normal rather than increasingly litigious. My friend, however, was concerned that I take every precaution. "Hopson," he said, "they're going after you."

Dealing with lawyers is complicated, tedious, and expensive. What a great thing it would be to go through our lives with as few dealings with them as possible. But I had to face reality; there was little choice in my case. This whole story was about the value of law, order, and integrity. I wanted it to protect people like Krista, but I also wanted it to protect people like me.

I needed to "lawyer up," then, for the purpose of protecting my chosen career.

What I needed was an attorney who specialized in both employment law and law enforcement. I didn't have to look too far before finding Bill Buckman. Among other successful accomplishments, he had taken on the New Jersey State Police for the racial profiling of drivers on the New Jersey Turnpike in the landmark case of State vs. Soto. The published opinion in that case became a benchmark in the area of racial profiling.

I packed a leather briefcase full of letters, timelines, and memorandums—so much paperwork stemming from one car stop just eleven days into my career. So many lives had been changed because one man abused justice and another refused to endorse it.

I traveled to the appropriate address and met the brillo-haired, bespectacled attorney whose accomplishments had impressed me. He greeted me with a warm smile and a soft handshake. His office was covered in glory—diplomas, certificates, awards, and commendations—but he couldn't have been more down to earth.

I told my story—how many times had I recounted it by now? Then I handed over my stack of evidence, the chronology, and the items that would most assist Buckman's research. He showed a vivid interest, and was impressed that I already had so much organized, documented information for him.

On a more informal basis, I told him the bottom line: I liked my job and didn't want to lose it. I also wanted to do what I could to change the culture of hazing within the State Police. Buckman nodded compassionately. These were roads he had traveled, issues he had faced. He understood the powers I was up against, and he also knew how to stand up to them.

The hour was well spent. Buckman carefully explained my options and showed me how to insulate myself from future acts of hazing and retaliation. That was no easy task, of course. Like everyone else, he urged caution. If I was going to stay the course, risks came with the territory. I thanked him, but I decided not to sign the agreement binding us together. I'm a deliberate person, careful with major decisions such as this one. I knew that I couldn't find a better advocate, but I still wanted time to mull it over.

I smiled, thanked Bill Buckman, and told him I'd be in touch.

I also consulted with my therapist during this time. He asked how things were going in my world, and I brought him up to speed on recent events. He sighed as he heard that my job was now on the line.

"I'm sure you realize," he said gently, "that you're likely to face an uphill climb for the duration of your career, as long as you stay in law enforcement. The culture is powerful. It wasn't built in a day, and it won't come down quickly either."

"You've counseled a few others in my shoes," I said. "Where are they now?"

"Not in uniform, most of them," he said. "Once they've come forward, they realize there are healthier places to spend their work days. I'm just telling you the way it is."

"So pretend you're me. What do you do?"

He looked at me for a moment, pursed his lips, and said, "I'd get out. Then I'd sue their pants off for what they did."

I walked to my car and thought, *It happened again. I'm more anxious in leaving than I was when I arrived.*

But I had issues to consider. That night I tossed and turned in bed as I thought about those words—"Sue their pants off." It would be no small commitment. The pile of documents would double, triple. I would be less involved with law enforcement and more with law, *period*. My fingers were on the lid of Pandora's box, knowing that once it was opened, and once the dark things inside flew out, there was no closing it again.

A few days later, I had processed the advice of Buckman and my counselor. I drove to the attorney's office and signed on with him. My mind was still racing, weighing options, as I parked my car and walked into the lobby. A part of me wanted to flee litigation—go to the other side of the world, return to a Hawaiian beach. But I'm not much for surrendering. You can call it persevering or you can call it plain old stubborn, but I wasn't going to back down.

As I signed my name yet again, I placed myself in the position of an adversary to the State of New Jersey and the New Jersey State Police. That very day, Buckman fired off a letter to the superintendent of the State Police, asking that my appearance before the re-enlistment board be rescinded. This is how I understood his purpose: simply protecting my job and creating a buffer against retaliation.

Chapter 9:

Big Brother Is Watching

Life moved on. I tried to nourish my soul by spending time with friends and family. I talked to my immediate family and, for the most part, received encouragement. I told them, "I wouldn't wish my situation on anyone." While some questioned my sanity and capacity to take on the State Police, my mother patiently reminded me that I was in this situation for a reason.

That was something I believed with all my heart. We may feel small and alone, but everything is for a reason, and God is in control. Even on the bad days, I continued to pray and ask God for the strength to forge ahead. In the long run, I saw those prayers answered. I may not have wished this course on others, but it was the cross I was determined to bear.

Challenges continued to come, but I felt myself rising to meet them. One day, just before a training seminar, I was sitting in a state police academy classroom when a fellow trooper walked up. He made a show of conversing with the trooper next to me, but another agenda became clear. He said, loud enough that I might hear, "How about those Lords of Discipline tee shirts they found in Tuckerton?" Subtlety wasn't his objective.

The LOD advocate waited a second for a reaction, but I merely turned calmly in his direction, holding my tongue. "Why hide from it?" he continued to my colleague. "We should start a LOD unit. On midnights, the guys who don't answer calls could ride with the Lords."

Message received—someone wanted me to know that the Lords of Discipline were alive and well. The guy walked away, and I noticed that the trooper sitting next to me was noticeably uncomfortable. I suppose he found that position, in the crossfire between the Lords and me, like being between a rock and a hard place. I looked at him and said, "It is what it is."

As the seminar got underway, the other guys took notes on the legal topic. I was writing down the details of the conversation that had just been directed my way. Later, a little investigation revealed that the LOD advocate was a state police union official, a respected member of the rank and file. At one time, an occurrence like this might have cost me an evening's sleep. I had come a certain distance, however, and my skin was a little thicker. I felt strangely comforted that they couldn't suppress my resolve. The law was on my side, and all they could do was engage in rounds of playground taunting, and flash their secret tee shirts.

The shirts, of course, were always an important piece of visual evidence. As the state often tried to make the case that there was no Lords of Discipline, the train of tee shirts told a different story.

A colleague once summoned me to meet him in an office within the barracks.

"I wanted to tell you something," he said, after making sure the door was closed. "I followed the court-martial, when you testified against _____." He named the sergeant at this point. "I spotted him at the National Trooper Coalition picnic in Delaware, wearing one of those tee shirts." Our conversation was in October of 2003.

"Right out in the open, eh?" I asked, shaking my head. "Did people stare at it at all?"

"All the top brass saw it, and no one raised an eyebrow—nobody except one official." And he named a high-ranking African American administrator. "I heard him order the sergeant to change his shirt. The guy just stared back at him, and then he ignored the command. He still had the shirt on later. Can you believe it?"

"Some things never change," I shrugged. "That's what I'm up against." To be honest, even after all that I had learned, I had a hard time believing that the Lords were that bold during such a tense time. They had to believe they were untouchable.

That kind of brazen confidence gave me pause. On another occasion, I hitched a ride with two veteran troopers to attend the annual police ethics seminar. These were two guys I worked with on a regular basis, and I respected their work ethic. During the ride, one of them looked at me and bellowed, "Hey, Hopson, you should be the one teaching the ethics class."

I smiled and replied, "Sir, I'm just trying to keep my job." We all had a good laugh, but I realized that I had become a kind of symbol. The sergeant stood for one thing, and I was the face of the opposition. Maybe I needed my own shirt that said, "I just want to keep my job."

Fighting for your career causes you to cherish it even more. There was probably no trooper who took his work more seriously than me, because I was paying a high price simply to show up and do it. If police work boiled down to one word, it would be *professionalism*. I wanted to apply the highest standards of conduct toward my co-workers and the general public, because I believed in that standard and also because I was under close scrutiny. My every move was probably being watched, so I'd better get things right.

I tried to treat everyone with respect, including the criminals I dealt with on a daily basis. I marveled at what a difference it made.

Take most serial offenders, people who have spent years in and out of the prison system; treat them with common respect, and you'll see their attitudes soften immediately. They cooperate much better, and that made my job easier. It would be hard to count the number of times someone thanked me, after the arrest sequence, simply for being fair with them.

There was the African American male, twenty, whom I transported to jail one hot summer night after a bank robbery. His record was a lengthy one: thefts, stick-ups, and burglaries. He was a professional himself, knowing the system inside out, knowing exactly how to work it. As we cruised down the highway, I glanced at him in the rearview mirror. Undaunted, unrepentant, he was staring out of the window. I turned down the radio and asked him, "Are you happy with how your life is turning out?"

He had the right to remain silent, and that's what he did. Just a slight shake of the head signified his response: *no.*

"Why are you choosing to live your life as a criminal?"

Small shrug of the shoulders.

"So what are you going to do when you get out of County?"

He met my glance within the mirror and spoke up. "I don't know how to do anything else than what I'm doin' right now."

"I don't believe that," I said. "I do believe we all have choices. So you could choose to turn your life around."

"Man, you don't know me."

"True. All I know about you is that you're making bad choices. Bro, there are easier ways to make money. Have you ever considered that you might be better than this?"

The conversation ended there. We arrived at the jail, where I escorted the prisoner and checked him in. I stood by as he was strip-searched and clothed in an orange jumpsuit. Just before he was taken to his cell, he began to walk in my direction with a question in his eyes. The two corrections officers, of course, took hold of him and pointed him toward the door.

The prisoner said, "Can I talk to the big man for a second?"

The officers looked at me and I nodded in affirmation. The inmate walked over and said, "I'll remember what you said. Thank you."

I whispered in his ear, "Keep your chin up." As they walked him into the corridor, he looked back one time, as if fixing my face in his memory. I have no doubt that, even with the number of arrests on his record, never once had anyone else taken the time to give him a single word of encouragement—a simple recognition that he was "better than this."

Maybe it made no difference. Perhaps it was a drop of soothing oil in an ocean of inflammation, and not a thing changed in the young man's life. I admit to often wondering about him, and wondering about the small nation of lives like his, being hardened daily on the wheel of institutional discipline. There's got to be a way to change a few of those lives.

Sometimes I would cruise the highways and byways on a cool evening and think, "This isn't a bad life." It was calm; there was opportunity for reflection or enjoying a starry sky; and of course there were regular opportunities to provide service to ordinary people. A stranded motorist might repeat his appreciation over and over. A lonely senior citizen might enjoy a friendly word. There were mornings when I stopped by the local school to visit with the students, hoping to provide some kind of positive role model as they considered what to do with the adulthood that beckoned.

My oath was to protect and to serve the public, and that second one was the one I enjoyed. But there was the other side, too. I parked my car in grass medians on the interstate highways, watching the radar as it clocked speeds. Sometimes I hid behind rows of overgrown bushes, seeing the ubiquitous minivans, driven by soccer moms, moving at warp speed to get their kids to practice on time.

When I was spotted, the brakes would slam, the cell phones would disappear, and the unfastened seat belts would click shut all at the same time. Why do people think we don't see?

On one nightshift, two "crotch-rocket" motorcycles were moving at 112 miles per hour on the interstate. I was heading north and passed them, going south. I steered into the grass and U-turned to the southbound side. I floored it, but I thought there was little to no chance to overtake those speed merchants. I was miles behind with the disadvantage of having to drive in a way that would not endanger the public.

I could see the speck ahead, growing smaller. Yet within several miles, the bikers began to slow down. They hadn't spotted me. Driving a slick-top patrol car, without overhead lights, I was inconspicuous—especially at night.

The bikers suddenly looked over their shoulder, not believing a car was pacing them from behind. I flashed the emergency lights and sounded the siren. One of the bikers rolled his head back, knowing he was pinched, and quickly pulled over.

I pulled behind the bikes, called in the stop to dispatch, and waited a minute before approaching. I eyed the bikers with a cold stare and asked, "Any idea how fast you were going?"

They shrugged their shoulders and shook their head, no.

I said, "Does 112 ring a bell?"

Their eyes winced as they stared downward, nodding sadly. One more joyride had become unexpectedly costly.

Troopers understand that most motorists who are pulled over are good people having bad days. Sometimes, however, we encounter irate drivers; those are the ones who test our patience. They're easy to pick out in traffic. These are the pilots with death-grips on the steering wheel and bulging jugular veins. Their cars may have slowed to a stop, but not their raging emotions. They will say things like, "Don't you have something better to do? Why not go and catch the *real* criminals?" Irate motorists tend to have a temporary lapse in judgment.

There's also the namedropper. The moment a police officer approaches the driver's window; the driver quickly begins recounting the important people he or she knows. The namedropper pulls out stickers, cards, or placards to prove it. This person obviously believes this will terrify the officer like a cross shown to a vampire, neatly warding off a traffic ticket.

I learned a lot about people simply by dealing with them as drivers of automobiles. But I learned the most in another sector of my job: in the investigations that were never solved.

Talk to a veteran law enforcement officer, and you'll find that he or she carries a mental file of unsolved cases. The unfinished business nags at them long after they retire. The fact that most people don't realize is that all across the country, most cases go unsolved. A car stereo is stolen from your dashboard overnight; someone with a hidden face robs a convenience store; an innocent bystander is shot in a drive-by shooting.

So many times there simply isn't enough evidence to push a case forward. The average police officer spends a certain amount of time in the stressful line of duty, and even more time inactive, simply waiting. Downtime is when cops get into trouble. What does an officer do with all the adrenalin from handling a domestic abuse case, or sorting through the remains of a fatal accident? He could be investigating a crime scene knowing that a dangerous assailant is hidden nearby.

Then he's back at the barracks, filled with nervous energy and nothing on which to expend it. The stress level for most of the 800,000 law enforcement officers in America fluctuates like a roller coaster. [6] There is the storm, and the calm on either ends of it. For

---

6   National Law Enforcement Officer Memorial Fund, www.nicomf.com, April
     3, 2006.

some reason no one grasps, there are people like me out there who are attracted to that lifestyle.

Law enforcement is the essential mark of a civilized society. We come together as communities and insist that some come out from among us to maintain order and protect citizens. Those volunteers are empowered as our police. We have a tiered system of law enforcement consisting of municipal, county, state, and federal organizations upholding thousands of laws throughout our country.

The challenge is a healthy flow of communications between all those levels, from federal down to the town sheriff. Sometimes there's even rivalry and competition. When communications break down, we see problems such as domestic and international terrorism. Our nation took a blow with the 9/11 attacks. There had been information, and dangerous individuals had been identified, but the information failed to run its course. Identified terrorists were allowed to board planes.

We've made improvements since then, but there are still problems when the federal government doesn't disseminate information down to every police jurisdiction. It could be bureaucratic red tape, unwillingness to share intelligence, inept procedure, or something else. The bottom line is that national security is at risk, and police officer safety is compromised.

Where am I going with this? I see no end in sight for terrorism, but there is something we can do to improve communications and training for all levels of law enforcement: we can nationalize America's police force.

An argument can be made that a national police force is unconstitutional. But it's illuminating to take note of Article 4, Section 4, of the Constitution:

The United States shall guarantee to every State in this Union a Republican Form of Government, and shall protect each of

them against Invasion: and on Application of the Legislature,
or of the Executive (when the legislature cannot be convened)
against domestic Violence.

Article 6 continues:

This Constitution, and the laws of the United States which shall
be made in Pursuance thereof, and all Treaties made, or which
shall be made, under the Authority of the United States, shall
be the supreme Law of the Land; and the Judges in every State
shall be bound thereby, any Thing in the Constitution or Laws
or Laws of any State to the Contrary not withstanding.

Legal minds will continue to debate whether a national police force is unconstitutional or not. Whether the framers of our constitution ever intended or even imagined such an idea, the fact remains that in today's world, it makes sense.

Our country now employs more than 200,000 people in the Department of Homeland Security alone. And according to the Department of Homeland Security, the U.S. has over 87,000 governmental jurisdictions at the local, state, and federal levels.

How can 87,000 governmental jurisdictions communicate and disseminate data efficiently? As it stands now, they can't and they don't. In order to streamline data, local, state, and federal jurisdictions should unite resources and manpower for the common good of our national security.

Nationalization would serve more than one purpose. Communications would immediately see drastic improvement. At the same time, we would experience the benefits of standardized training for all law enforcement officers. Training academies nationwide would require officers to maintain academic, physical, and ethical requirements so that officers in Flint, Michigan would be as competent as those found in Phoenix, Arizona. Such standardized training would create cohesiveness and impede the power play of jurisdictional authority. This would clearly enhance officer safety and morale. Subcultures such as the Lords of Discipline or acts of hazing would be treated as pariah and detrimental to morale.

One comprehensive set of laws and standard operating procedures (SOPs) should be set forth and supported by Congress. The SOPs should be fair and reasonable with no room for misinterpretation. Officers who are trained and tested both practically and academically should be able to enforce the laws and SOPs in any city or state, thus eliminating bureaucratic red tape and clearly defining law and order.

Any certified police officer with probable cause should be able to pull a car over, effect an arrest for a RICO violation, or even check the cargo of trains and planes. United States Police Forces should be in charge of all security for appropriate events and venues. Officers should have state-of-the-art equipment at their fingertips to retrieve relevant data such as wanted persons, citizenship, Amber alerts, and license status.

Though a United States Police Force is a bold and radical option; our nation should consider any reasonable measure that will make it stronger and safer. No one questions the need for national military forces, as opposed to local militia. In unity there is strength and streamlined efficiency. Is it really unthinkable that we could take the same approach to domestic law and order? A prominent and professional national police force would gain the respect of Americans, just as we revere the U.S. Army, Navy, Air Force, and Marines. At the same time terrorists would know they were up against a substantially tougher opponent.

Chapter 10:

Taking Care of Business

As two fresh-faced young troopers complete their training and proudly allow the badge to be pinned to their caps, they have every reason to be excited.

The trooper has come to this moment on the threshold of a new career, because it is the life work she has chosen. The rookie officer believes with all his heart in law, order, and integrity. She is there to make the world a safer and a better place.

He takes immaculate care of his uniform. She polishes the badge not because there is anything intrinsically valuable or even unique about the small wedge of metal—but because of what it symbolizes. He is young, energetic, in the best shape of his life, and in the prime of his years. She has elected to make a free gift of them to the world and the citizenry around her. He could be paid better in other professions. She could be physically safer and freer from stress. But if those things were all that mattered to them, they would be in some other field, doing some other thing.

The young troopers feel an equal pull from the past and the future. From the past, she feels a strong attraction to the tradition of law enforcement—the "blue wall" that remains unbroken, the line of men and women who stand guard on the wall. He sees the pictures of officers from decades past, and he wants to measure up to the unspoken standard. She looks forward to fitting in with those brothers and sisters in the department; to bonding with them through the trials and tribulations ahead; to swapping pictures of children as families are built; to standing down someday, with honor and distinction, and passing the badge to those who come behind him, extending the blue wall a few decades farther.

But there is a pull from the future, too. He brings with him the technology of his time: state-of-the-art breathalyzers, forensic science, DNA, mobile video recording devices, the latest guns and ammo, and whatever else is new at any given time. She realizes she's a bit more comfortable with the newest innovations than the veterans. He also believes, deep in his heart, that he will "raise the bar" when it comes to moral and ethical standards. Her young generation can help to usher in reform and renewal. He's heard a rumor or two about the way things are among some of the more experienced troopers. He knows about racial profiling, for example, and about the kind of officer who brings a personal agenda instead of a clear-minded, objective sense of duty.

Like the new graduate entering any profession, what she lacks in experience she makes up for in "by the book" knowledge, fresh from class training. The regulations are clear and authoritative, so he respects them.

The new trooper isn't completely naïve; she knows what real-world police culture is like. At least he believes he has a good idea about its nature. And if she thought bad habits were permanent, ingrained, or indelible, again she would likely make some other career choice. We all believe we can leave our mark.

I'm certain that few—if any—officers, troopers, sheriffs, or agents enter the ranks of law enforcement with the idea of playing a helpless role in a culture of corruption. No, most feel the pull of a brighter future as well as a hallowed past. Being young and idealistic, they believe all things are possible. The new generation will keep the best of the old times and discard the worst. Yet, with the aid of New School technology and Old School dedication—a new generation of tireless public servants arise.

The assumptions above, I believe, provide the starting point for a newly trained officer. What he discovers is something entirely different.

An ingrained culture can run very deep within a community of workers. Certain beliefs and traditions are quietly, discretely enforced, and anyone who goes against the grain will find out just how high and how solid the blue wall can be. At that point, the idealistic young officer has a choice to make. Just how important are these values? Important enough to stick his neck out? Enough to feel the chill of a roomful of disapproving veterans, who have power and numbers?

Many, of course, fall quickly into line. Psychologists and sociologists have studied the phenomenon of peer pressure and "herd mentality" for many years. In a number of experiments, they've demonstrated that people make moral decisions in a group context quite differently than they do in private. For example, if someone has fallen on the sidewalk, and Joe is the only person passing by, he is more likely to stop and help. If there are many others passing by, and no one is helping, then Joe himself is less likely to help. His sense of personal responsibility is lessened by the presence of others.

In other words, when people find themselves in a group, and particularly if they want to be well accepted in that group, they will modify their behavior—sometimes in ways counter to what they actually believe, how they have been trained, or what society has told them is right. When they witness an occurrence that doesn't seem right, they will feel deep anxiety, but—being new in the group— they may lack the confidence to speak up. In time their anxiety will surface, as they grow morally calloused. They'll say, "Everybody does this. Why rock the boat?"

The herd mentality is powerful among law enforcement officers. Police wear uniforms for a reason; uniformity is valued. There is incredible resistance to change or renewal. A wiry old trooper once told me that the New Jersey State Police would never change. He had been around for some time, and that was his firm belief. I didn't realize it at the time, nor did I wish to believe it—but he had good reason to make such a statement.

It's true that African-Americans and women were integrated into what was once the exclusive domain of white males. This happened only because the federal government required it. This is another reason that I've come to the decision that a nationalized police makes sense—the "blue wall" that extends, unbroken, from your local police district to the highest offices in our nation. Sometimes the power of national authority is the only thing that makes change happen. The federal government had to intervene in the South during the 1960s, during the Civil Rights movement. Presidents Johnson and Kennedy invoked the option of calling out the National Guard.

It also took action in Washington, D.C. for something to be done about racial profiling among the New Jersey State Police. The federal government began monitoring the dismantling of those practices that had become habits of law enforcement.

Ultimately, in my view, the blame must be laid at the door of the New Jersey State Police administration. I've heard it referred to as a "revolving door of empty suits." I'm far from the first to observe that the bureaucracy holds a small population of officials who draw the highest salaries for accomplishing the least results—and of course, most of us would agree that New Jersey is far from unique in that regard.

Meanwhile, most of the men and women who wear the uniforms, patrol the streets, and solve the crimes are hard-working and upstanding. State troopers nobly serve and protect the public, and I will always believe that it is a privilege to wear the uniform. However, my indoctrination into the New Jersey State Police also brought me to the observation of corruption within the ranks and the condoning of it by the bureaucracy.

My great challenge was to carry out all the implications involved in confronting it, while still doing my everyday job with the highest standards. As the Lords of Discipline matter continued to unfold, I focused on my work—particularly the new and engrossing adventure of working with Detective Everson in the area of criminal investigation.

One day after work, Detective Everson talked to me about another case. He and I made our way to State Police headquarters and met with a lieutenant from the missing persons unit. He directed our attention to a particularly disturbing case involving a missing teenage girl. After twenty-five years, the missing persons unit had elected to revisit the evidence. We were briefed on the basic facts, provided hundreds of file documents, and asked to begin investigating the matter.

The next day, I received the order to come off regular patrol and report to the barracks. I was again temporarily assigned to the detective bureau, back to plainclothes. There I was given an unmarked car and provided with a voluminous case file. It was, in fact, a "cold case"—an old, unsolved crime.

As I read through the files, my imagination traveled back to 1979, when a sixteen-year-old girl had disappeared one night after a high school party. I was a small child in those days; I thought about a family going this long without any sense of closure when a precious child seemed to vanish from the face of the earth. The missing teenager had allegedly been raped, bludgeoned to death, and then thrown into a sludge lagoon. Yet there was no *corpus delecti*—no physical body in evidence.

I was able to read through the interview notes and familiarize myself with the suspects and witnesses. All of the victim's friends would now be entering middle age. I traveled to the alleged crime scene and had my own conversation with a confidential informant. Then I coordinated a fresh search for the victim's remains. I made use of State Police resources along with NecroSearch, a non-profit organization specializing in searching for clandestine gravesites and evidence. I contacted this group based on its reputation and advanced technologies.

My case hinged on bones, and on the remote chance that they could still be recovered. The goal was not only to solve the missing persons case, but also to gain some degree of closure for the family after nearly twenty-five years.

I experienced something typical for a detective: I all but lost myself in an old, nearly forgotten case. All crimes offer us mysteries we're eager to solve, but a cold case has a special power to it. For one thing, we know that previous detectives have already come up short, and the questions remain. So there is a heightened challenge to succeed by picking up the pieces of an unsolved puzzle.

Second, the element of history makes it compelling. We meet the witnesses and suspects, now in their middle years, and imagine them as teenagers. We think about the fact that there is probably someone walking this earth who has carried the deep secret for all these years. Maybe he or she has committed some other crime and been imprisoned—but this particular debt has never been paid. That proposition is unacceptable to those who believe in a just society.

I was consumed with the case of the missing girl. The interviews began again—a dozen of them—and in one case, I had a wiretap set up to capture a furtive conversation. A search and recovery effort was made once again. I was absolutely determined to solve this case.

But I made a crucial error.

I was new at this, of course. Detective Everson knew that, and I'm grateful he was willing to believe in my abilities—but I overlooked a crucial detail. I got permission to perform the wiretapping, but I didn't get a written time extension from the county prosecutor to keep it going. It may seem like a technicality, but I knew the standards for procedure were the highest in this kind of matter. If a suspect were brought to trial, any little evidentiary problem would present an opportunity for a defense attorney. Evidence isn't admissible unless it has been legally obtained.

And of course, I had already staked my career on a battle for integrity and adherence to proper procedure. I couldn't be a hypocrite. After meeting with the prosecutor, we decided the case couldn't be compromised; I relinquished it, with all the new evidence gathered, to another detective.

It was one more point of tension for me. I felt a real connection to this case but I made an error. I understood why I needed to walk away from it, but it still hurt.

Outside the country prosecutor's office, I got involved in a verbal confrontation with my successor. The new detective on the case made an insulting remark about my error, and I didn't take his words lightly. A heated conversation ensued. At one point the detective said, "I don't know about your past, but . . ."

I cut him off. "What does my past have to do with this case?"

"Get a grip on yourself, detective."

I grabbed my briefcase and turned to walk away. I didn't need to let the war of words escalate any further. I climbed into my unmarked police car and took a couple of breaths, staring straight ahead and letting my heartbeat slow down. I was truly angry with myself over the procedural error. It would have been so easy to get that extension—just a telephone call and routine paperwork, while I had been making genuine strides in solving a crime one quarter of a century old.

I drove back to the barracks and submitted all my investigative work and criminal leads. Whether I could be a part of the team or not, I still hoped the truth could be found. The victim's parents, family, and friends deserved it.

As for me, I hoped another opportunity would come my way. Sometimes it takes the pain of our errors to learn valuable lessons; I would be that much more cautious and vigilant next time. Surely I had shown I had the energy, drive, and intuition to be an effective investigator.

Some would say I received a level of redemption when I was given several commendations based upon my contributions to that case. But there was no personal consolation for me in those. Above all, I saw that the case itself remained unsolved. We made strides, but close simply doesn't count. In a perfect world, our police forces would solve every single crime, and no transgression would go unpunished. No parents would lie awake wondering about the identity and whereabouts of the monster that stole their child.

But this isn't a perfect world. Nor was I a perfect detective. At the end of that experience, I vowed to work to live, rather than live to work. I was more than just a police officer. I was a complex human being who needed a full and balanced life, so I was going to have to learn to compartmentalize these areas. During the day, I should be fully focused on being the best public servant I could be. When the workday ended, however, I needed to walk away and live my life, pursue my other interests, and nurture my friendships.

I wanted to avoid becoming burned out. Now more than ever, I needed to be a marathon runner who paced himself, rather than a sprinter who gave all that he had in one brief rush.

Chapter 11:

Critical Mass

P riority one for me was to be a catalyst for change in the culture of the New Jersey State Police. It wasn't about being vindictive, or winning a cash settlement, or any selfish motive. I simply wanted the assurance that measures for reform would be undertaken. The state government needed to show a sincere effort to clean up the culture that allowed the Lords of Discipline, or any similar group, to cast their toxic shadow over law enforcement in our state.

I had rested my hopes in the power of going public—of shedding light on the darker corners of this culture. But I wasn't the first to fail in such an attempt. Once again, the New Jersey Attorney General's Office demonstrated that it lacked the will to do what would best serve its citizens. Through my attorney, Bill Buckman, we made several good-faith attempts to establish negotiation with the State Police toward the goal of reform. All of these fell through. Therefore, with reluctance, we filed a federal lawsuit (03cv5817) based upon the violation of my civil rights.

We asserted that my constitutional rights, based upon the first and fourteenth amendments, had been violated. The lawsuit described how the Lords of Discipline targeted me after refusing to falsify the facts surrounding an illegal arrest. The twenty-five-page lawsuit outlined the principles and demands, which clarified why I blew the whistle.

I found it incredible that the Attorney General would allow such a publicly damaging lawsuit to be filed, rather than simply doing what should have been done even without the threat of public exposure. If significant and lasting changes could have been quietly made, I would have been more than pleased; I certainly had no desire to undermine the good name of New Jersey State Troopers. It was something like having a family member arrested—it had to be done, but I would have gone to almost any length to avoid it. However, I wouldn't go to the length of letting the state protect a culture of corruption.

The first amendment protects free speech. Officers associated with the Lords of Discipline had attempted to deny me the right to speak out and tell the truth. The fourteenth amendment establishes equal protection under the law. As a United States citizen, I was entitled to full protection by the government and those working in its name. I could not be singled out for different treatment because of race, creed, or beliefs—in this case, for my belief in honest police reports, and my insistence upon carrying out our work by the proper standard operating procedures.

As I arrived home at my apartment that evening, I fixed a small dinner and relaxed a bit. I finally had a chance to let it all sink in: the full gravity of a lawsuit against the state. Two and a half years ago, I couldn't have imagined it. Even a few months ago, it still would have been hard to believe. Like many people, I had assumed that our governmental agencies are composed of men and women with strong ideals, who are eager to root out wrongdoing wherever it is found in their jurisdiction. Just showing them the problem should be sufficient. Having to contest the issue in court was inconceivable to me.

I don't like litigation; I don't know many people who do. Certainly there should be much less of it in today's world. But there are times when the law is our only recourse, and we must use the system for worthy and unselfish goals. I knew this was such a time. The state had harbored the negative, lawless culture of the Lords of Discipline for twenty years or more. My counselor and my legal counsel bore testimony to the fact that others before me had been trampled and abused by dark forces within the system. But even if I failed, and even if I knew in advance that I couldn't succeed, I still had to do what was right. Maybe this time we would get it done. My hope was to end hazing in the State Police so that no other troopers would be victimized.

The headlines appeared the next day: "Trooper Accuses State Police of Harassment."

The lawsuit was covered in detail, and it wasn't long before the op-ed pages chimed in. One was entitled "State Police Bad Boys," with its writer highly critical of the State Police administration as well as the attorney general's office.

I was due to report for the nightshift, so I had the day to worry about the reception I would receive when I came in. I walked in and made my way to the locker room to change, but strangely enough, no one raised the issue. As a matter of fact, no one talked at all; the silence made its own comment. It was my decision to go forward with the lawsuit, and I was resolved to live with the consequences.

I went about my duties for more than a week without incident. My fellow troopers kept me at arm's length, but I wasn't targeted or challenged in any way. Then, ten days after filing the suit, I received the inevitable phone call—I was being transferred again. Call it "Musical Barracks." Go in circles while the music plays, settle in one space, then the music starts all over again.

I knew that settling in could prove a greater challenge this time. When I had come from Tuckerton, there had been whispers; now there were headlines and editorials. I could be seen at this point—fairly or not—as an aggressive troublemaker, a trooper with a lawyer who was trying to cash in.

More worrisome still was the news about where I was going. My destination was a barracks already caught up in an internal affairs investigation. It concerned hazing and sexual harassment. What was the message here? I was the public face of hazing, so headquarters decided to transfer me to a barracks where hazing had been identified. There was only one conclusion to be drawn from this action: The powers-that-be just raised the temperature.

I wasn't going to go down that easily. I called my attorney immediately, and he requested that the State Police rescind the transfer order. It was clear to us that the state was trying to get under my skin, but they were holding a two-edged sword. Whatever they used against me could later be used against them in the public eye.

As all these things occurred, the Christmas carols were beginning to play. I began to see tinsel and wreaths, and folks on their way to holiday parties. I was already receiving Christmas "gifts" on a regular basis—prank phone calls late at night. Instead of eggnog and fruitcake, I was swallowing an increased dosage of antidepressant medication.

It was a blue Christmas to be sure. On Christmas Eve, at a family gathering, relatives asked why they hadn't heard from me. I politely apologized and told them it had been a particularly busy year. There was no way I was going to give them the details. Maybe they could read their newspapers a little more closely. My father did, however, follow the news and warned, "You can't beat the state police, Justin. What you're doing won't make a difference."

Some state troopers, of course, have to work on Christmas Day. I began my shift by emptying my locker and slowly peeling off photographs taped to the inside of the door. I loaded my things into a patrol car and said goodbye to my colleagues before leaving for my new assignment. Many of them, of course, were good people who would have liked to support me. I'm sure I always had a certain amount of silent approval from men and women who wanted to see things change, and who hated hazing as much as me—but who had spouses and children, perhaps, or some other reason they chose not to fight the establishment.

Across the wintry roads, I headed for my new barracks. What little traffic I saw was mostly families, heading from one warm hearth to another, sharing a carefree holiday cheer that I really missed, and hadn't enjoyed for three straight seasons. As they sat over feasts of ham or turkey, I stopped in a lonely café to order a hot chocolate. I sat in my car, sipping it and contemplated my future.

Finally I came to my new barracks, where a few troopers were on duty. I made several brief introductions, hoping to make the best possible impression. By the time I filled out some necessary paperwork, it was time to leave for the evening. I sighed as I thought about pushing the great stone up the hill one more time: new highways and byways to learn, a new cast of colleagues to vet, and a new round of questions from internal affairs to answer. I could only hope that the transition wouldn't be too stressful.

The next morning a lieutenant called me on my cell phone. My transfer had been rescinded. We'd gotten our wish, of course, but not before packing up and moving on Christmas Day. It was already time to do it all over again. As with the re-enlistment board hearing, the transfer order itself was rescinded. This meant I could go back to the barracks I'd just left. Was the state backing down, if only a little bit? Sure, they'd yanked my chain. They'd let me know where I was in the pecking order.

But I was determined not to be cynical. Why not take this at face value? I had been heading for a barracks under the shadow of investigation for sexual harassment and hazing. I was now being allowed to stay where I had grown comfortable. If the state was really taking off the gloves, they would insist on transferring me somewhere new and making me be the "new kid on the block" yet again.

As I sighed in gratitude over those thoughts, internal affairs called. They wanted to set up a meeting to discuss my lawsuit. We set a time, and I was even promised that no more transfers lay in my foreseeable future. Again, I said a silent prayer of thanks.

Three days later, I was transferred.

My last vestiges of optimism drained away. Now I could call things what they were without any question of cynicism. The State Police administration felt it had absolutely nothing to lose by pulling my strings, making me dance, and wearing me down. They had no fear—this could go on forever, and they wanted me to know that.

I continued to consult my counsel, but I also sought advice in other places. For example, I spoke to a retired Philadelphia police officer I had known for years. He was familiar with what was happening in my life, and his prescription was simple: "At this rate, Justin, you'll never make it to retirement. You need to get out, and get out now."

Others near and dear to me agreed. With all that was going on, I had to fight to keep a two-year relationship alive with my girlfriend. I was transferred on a whim; I was on medication for anxiety; and I was losing sleep, if not because of worry, at least because of prank phone calls at terrible hours. My girlfriend knew I was in a bad place emotionally, and she wondered if both of us would be better off if we broke off our relationship.

That wasn't what I wanted—I needed all the love and support I could find at the moment, and I cared deeply about her. We sat together in the guest room of my home one evening, trying to sort it all out.

"I'm sorry for all this," I said, and she knew I meant it. "I know my work has gotten in the way. I haven't wanted that to happen—I haven't wanted it to have a negative impact on me or on our relationship—but I've had to do what I thought was right."

She told me that she was mainly worried about my well-being. She knew I had potential, and we had potential together. But the state and its harassment were beginning to take their toll on her, too.

I tried to explain. "I feel things slipping away," I said, fighting tears. "My career is spiraling downward, and I can't seem to do a thing to stop that from happening." With a shaky voice, I continued, "Our relationship is worth fighting for. But I just can't give you what you need right now."

"I know," she said quietly, wiping a tear from my cheek.

I let my head sink into my hands and tried to regain my composure. I couldn't think of anything else to say. But I felt her warm arms wrap around me as she whispered, "I just want my boyfriend back."

In January of 2004 I reported for the nightshift at the new barracks. The barracks was a forty-five minute drive, north of my home. I quickly met most of the troopers I'd be working with, and we cordially exchanged names and handshakes.

First up was a briefing about the night's agenda. A middle-aged sergeant attempted to conduct the meeting. But a trooper named Rickers quickly interrupted him. "Hey, Sarge," he said. "Better watch what you say. We've got a money-hungry trooper with us now, and he's suing us." In the course of the briefing, he made several other comments about me, leaving no uncertainty about his distaste for the "traitor" in the room.

I maintained my standard approach of sitting with my eyes glued to the front, registering no emotion. If you give in, the bullies win. Regardless, I could feel every eye in the room on me. Everyone was giving me the once-over after Rickers' blunt "advice." I found him to be an old school, disgruntled trooper who generally upheld the status quo.

Well, so much for making a good first impression. Trooper Rickers had eliminated any possibility that I might avoid awkwardness or controversy in my new location. I tried to keep a stiff upper lip, but the truth was that I had become overly sensitive to the remarks and opinions of fellow troopers. My once thick skin had worn down a layer or two, and I developed the tendency to isolate myself to avoid more displays similar to what Rickers had initiated. If they weren't going to leave me alone, maybe I could leave them alone.

I did what I'd kept on doing from the beginning. I worked hard, but something was different now. I knew I was becoming overwhelmed by all of it—the state jerking me around, the other troopers refusing to give me a chance, the need for lawyers, therapists, and pills. I was burning out quickly, and I knew it. I began to wonder if I had reached my limit. How many blows would it take before I threw in the towel and looked for some other job?

Perhaps the last straw occurred within ten days after I reported to my new barracks. I walked in and found an internal affairs lieutenant waiting for me. He introduced himself as Lieutenant Belfort and asked to interview me about my lawsuit.

Other troopers were all around, and naturally they were paying close attention. I could imagine what they were thinking. The lieutenant and I proceeded to an adjacent room for the interview.

As we got underway, I elected to have a police union representative present, as was my right. Lieutenant Belfort handed me a short stack of forms to sign, then kicked up his tattered, black leather shoes on the desk between us. He surveyed me dispassionately as I read and signed the forms of consent. When I finished, he loosened his tie and raised his chin, freeing his thick neck above the restrictive collar. I thought, *This guy is limbering up. He's getting ready to throw some curveballs.*

Yet he started with a few softballs—easy questions that simply established some basic facts. As the interview proceeded, however, he began to mix in some key issues regarding the specifics of the lawsuit. He would circle around a topic, returning to it to ask the same question in a different way. I kept close to the facts, explaining who, what, and why. Where necessary I stated that my attorney could best clarify something at issue.

Belfort listened to my answers, nodded thoughtfully, and occasionally glanced over at a tape recorder. It was a subtle reminder that everything was going on the tape, and could be used as evidence against me; whatever came out of my mouth could not be unsaid.

Finally there were no more questions in his arsenal. Lieutenant Belford asked me if I had any of my own, or any general comments.

I paused to collect my thoughts. Then I said, "Sir, the leadership of the New Jersey State Police has turned a blind eye to the Lords of Discipline. That group has been allowed to exist within the ranks for decades. That's what this is all about. And I have one other comment."

"What's that, Trooper?"

"I don't appreciate being lied to by internal affairs, and I don't enjoy having to work for people I cannot trust. Look, I had no choice but to file a lawsuit."

I'd answered the questions, made my statement, and so it was over. Belfort turned off the tape recorder. Then he had something he wanted to tell me off the record. I braced myself.

"Trooper, the fact is that several of your past supervisors have spoken very highly of your work ethic. They also say you're tight as a drum."

Fair enough. I allowed myself a little smile. "Sir," I said, "walk a mile in my shoes after blowing the whistle on corruption, and I predict you'll be tight as a drum as well."

He nodded and dismissed me.

Once again, I needed to calm my nerves. Life isn't much fun when you know a team of lawyers is somewhere framing questions to trip you up.

The lieutenant had heard correctly. I wasn't very loose or relaxed, and in the next few days I found myself becoming despondent. I needed my antidepressants, and it was harder than ever to get out of bed in the morning, wondering who or what was waiting for me at the barracks this time. I can remember simply lying on the bedroom floor at one point, my tears being dried by the wind of a ceiling fan just above me. I stared at the fan, its blades revolving as quickly as my thoughts. *God, why are you allowing this to happen to me? Please give me strength to carry on, Lord!*

Not long ago, intense, if draining, work focus had been my salvation. Chasing speeders, investigating accidents, responding to a domestic dispute, and answering a fire alarm was a good days work. But now I was finding I couldn't concentrate. I reached out to doctors and a few loved ones for advice. Their consensus was too much in agreement for me to ignore it. I decided to step away from the job for a while. My doctors compiled medical reports recommending an administrative leave of absence.

The State Police doctor briefed me on how this kind of thing works. Such a leave isn't a "get out of jail free" card. There are restrictions, such as being at home Monday through Friday between the hours of 9:00 AM to 5:00 PM. I would need authorized permission to leave my home for any reason.

I set my jaw and prepared to feel like a prisoner in my own home. Was this kind of isolation really the best thing for my emotional state? Was it the precise thing that my friends and loved ones had in mind? No more than an hour or two into my newly established administrative leave, a State Police lieutenant arrived at my house and asked me to voluntarily surrender my gun. The lieutenant also instructed me not to assume any police responsibilities from that moment onward. I thought, *They think I'll shoot myself. They see me as a liability, and don't want me representing them.*

The lieutenant saw my sadness and reluctance as I signed a form relinquishing my police responsibilities. She said, "I know this is difficult for you." She took my hand before turning to leave. I bolted the door behind her and wondered how long the days were going to seem. I had placed myself under house arrest.

The State Police were serious about these restrictions. They checked on me through telephone calls, certified mail, and occasional visits, always making sure I was home. It was difficult not to become a little paranoid about measures like those. On one occasion, I happened to be looking out my front window one afternoon as a black truck pulled in front of my house. Someone sitting in the cab began taking pictures of my home. I walked outside immediately to question the driver, but the driver quickly stepped on the accelerator the moment he saw my door open. I stood and watched the truck vanish around a corner.

Days turned into weeks and weeks turned into months as I paced from one room to another. I tried to watch some movies and read some books, but it was hard to get interested in much of anything. I wanted to be stimulated in some positive way, so I turned to self-help books and watched tapes of motivational speakers. None of them quite got through to me. Creeping boredom, discontent, and restlessness made a dangerous cocktail. Soon my friends, whom I needed more than ever, didn't seem to be available. The relationship I once had with my father ceased as I lost his support. As if things weren't bad enough, my girlfriend and I broke up, and I was single once again.

Chapter 12:

With a Little Help From My Friends

I was a prisoner inside my home—inside my emotions, really. It seemed as if my life had been filed away and forgotten by the powers that be. It felt as if I was on an island, and the world was moving on without me.

In that world, however—there were new and interesting developments.

Some of it was far away. The CIA admitted there were no weapons of mass destruction to be found in Iraq. I saw newly released photographs of Iraqi prisoners at Abu Ghraib, a detention facility. According to a U.S. military report, they were victims of "purposeless sadism." Nearly one hundred cases of abuse surfaced, including thirty-nine prisoner deaths. I ground my teeth as I heard a few commentators pass it all off as "fraternity-like hazing." That was a subject I knew something about. When people are dying, being sexually humiliated, and when their religion is being mocked, I struggle to see how that can be compared to frat house antics.

Other events weren't far away at all. In our own state, during that summer of 2004, a scandal emerged at the state capitol. Governor James McGreevey abruptly resigned from office as details came to light about his extramarital homosexual affair. His lover was threatening to file a lawsuit filled with intimate details.

The governor was twice married and the father of two children, so this development was tailor-made for the tabloid-driven news media. McGreevey was telling the world, through the reach of television, that he was a gay man living a lie.

Beyond the revelations of his personal life, there were more immediate concerns. He had appointed his male lover to be New Jersey's Homeland Security Advisor, a key position that drew $110,000 in annual salary. This was despite the man's lack of credentials for a job that involved the basic safety of every citizen in the state.

This shocking violation of the public trust, needless to say, brought about McGreevey's political downfall. The state GOP chairman declared that McGreevey was "a disgrace" to the state. Not for the first time, national media pundits were describing New Jersey as the most corrupt state in the union.

I had to wonder how the timing of this news event would affect my own conflict. The two stories were connected by state corruption. We had a governor misusing his powers of appointment, and we also had an attorney general who refused to clean up serious problems in his police force. The state was reeling from bad publicity, so the last thing New Jersey needed was another damaging news account, or a possible sordid story for *People* magazine.

I was thinking it all over at an Italian restaurant when I ran into Stefano, one of my closest friends. Stefano owned and operated the restaurant, which I frequented both on and off duty. As usual, he plunked himself down at my table and began to give me advice that pulled no punches. "Justin," he said, "You want to clean up the State Police?"

"That's the idea," I said.

"Well, my question to you is, how much do you want it? Are you ready to get dirty?"

I dug my fork into the entrée in front of me and let out a sigh. "If you mean going rogue, the answer is no," I said.

"I don't really mean that," he said. "There's no one less likely to go rogue than you. I'm talking about going for the jugular—with the rules."

"What do you mean?"

"That's for you to figure out. I mean, New Jersey's looking bad enough right now, correct? They don't need this little police problem. Last thing they want is a lot of tall headlines with the public learning all about something called 'The Lords of Discipline.' They want this thing to go away."

"So?"

"Don't give them the time to get their ducks in a row. Hit them while they're back on their heels. Keep them off balance. You'll know how to do it."

I hated the very thought of "getting dirty," however it translated. But I knew Stefano was speaking from a real-world perspective. He knew me well, he knew the facts of the case, and he also knew how formidable my opponent was. Therefore he didn't want me to show up at a gunfight with a dull knife.

I looked across the table at Stefano. Why was he so impassioned about this advice? He was a friend, sure, but there was something else. He was sick of what was going on. He was sick of averting his gaze, and watching everyone else do the same thing until nobody felt clean, everybody sharing part of the burden of guilt. He wanted someone to step up and do something, and if it didn't work—how long until someone else came along? Maybe never.

"These guys need to pay!" hissed Stefano, barely stifling his voice. I looked around nervously, hoping we weren't building an attentive audience.

In those days, I was used to looking around, watching my own back.

There was truth to what my friend said. If I wanted to make a heroic but useless gesture, that was one thing; but to bring about change—and that, of course, was the whole point of all this pain and grief—then *I had to play for keeps.*

If the vast disruption to my life amounted to no more than a futile gesture, I would never have been able to live with myself. I could make the sacrifice as long as I believed I was going to reach a goal that served others—namely to force the State Police to police itself.

Yes, the more I thought about it, Stefano had it right. I shouldn't be sitting in my home watching motivational speakers and brooding over my life. I needed to get mentally in gear, figuring out how to be proactive about the ends I wanted to accomplish.

I began to think about how I could seize the moment to leverage the state's weak public position against genuine reform in the police force. Maybe I could make some noise by speaking out publicly, or even get the American Civil Liberties Union involved. Everyone knows the ACLU can create problems for institutions reluctant to do the right thing.

I couldn't really see myself making either move. Several days later, at home, I sat on the sofa and weighed the possibilities. I wondered what the advice of a truly powerful person would be—someone who understood New Jersey and its politics?

I decided to write a prominent New Jersey senator whom I suspected would be sympathetic to my cause. In the letter, I outlined my case, focusing on the lack of meaningful reform in the problem of hazing within the ranks of the State Police. I attached the press release about the attorney general's investigation into the group. My three written letters and three telephone calls to the senator's office continued for weeks—until an indelible impression was made.

My letters must have made some kind of impression. The senator fired off a memo to the attorney general expressing deep concern about the matter of the Lords of Discipline. He described his displeasure that such a thing had ever been allowed to exist, calling it a "modern-day SS" within our state law enforcement agency (referring to the Nazi party's notorious Gestapo police force). Wow. That was some strong language.

I couldn't help but smile a little bit. It was nice to have a heavy hitter go to bat for me, someone who cast a shadow large enough to overwhelm all the little tyrants in my world. Meanwhile, the attorney general couldn't have been pleased to see a state senator getting worked up about a discussion the state wanted to quietly stifle.

Then I did something a little more creative. I summoned my courage and contacted Frank Serpico.

If that name rings a bell, you may have been a moviegoer back in the 1970s, or you might have seen the film *Serpico* on television since then. He's an icon who stood up against corruption, particularly in law enforcement. Al Pacino played him to perfection in the 1973 film.

Frank Serpico became a patrolman for the New York City Police Department in 1960. After walking a beat in the 81st precinct, he was promoted to the Bureau of Criminal Identification, where he spent two years filing fingerprints and carrying out other office tasks. Then he got his wish, which was to become a plainclothes cop in Brooklyn and the Bronx.

That's where he began to see things that shocked and infuriated him.

His job was to expose vice racketeering, but he frustrated the network of police officers around him, simply because he wouldn't take part in the widespread distribution of cash payoffs. At first, he refused the money while trying to go about his job as if it weren't happening. But he understood that approach was not sustainable. In time, he knew he needed to do something about the corruption he saw—even though his life would be placed at risk.

In 1967, Serpico wrote a report offering evidence of the illegal activity of his colleagues. As always, mountains of red tape, bureaucracy, and institutional apathy countered his challenge.

Then he found a kindred spirit named David Durk, and they began to fight police corruption together. But Serpico began to worry about surveillance, and he came to believe there was nothing he and his friend could do or say within the police department that wasn't going to be found out. Then it would be a matter of time before retribution occurred. He decided to go to the newspaper in an attempt to gain a little life insurance. The idea was that there was safety in the public eye.

On April 25, 1970, *The New York Times* ran a front-page story on the problem of corruption in the police department, and Frank Serpico was a focal point of the report. Mayor John Lindsay was forced to appoint a blue-ribbon panel to investigate the allegations. That panel became the Knapp Commission.

In February of 1971, four officers responded to a tip that a drug deal was going to happen at a certain location in Brooklyn. At the bust, Serpico was shot under circumstances that were extremely suspicious.

With the four cops arriving at the scene, two of them stayed in the car, one was posted in front of the apartment where the heroin deal was taking place, and Serpico watched from a fire escape. He then followed the two teenagers who had bought the drugs, as they walked down the stairs to the street.

The teens were arrested, and Serpico, who had heard the password for a drug buy, was ordered to go back and make a fake purchase to get the door open; then the other cops would rush in.

Three officers waited on the landing while Serpico knocked on the door. When the door opened a few inches, with the chain still connected, Serpico pushed at it with his shoulder and attempted to force his way into the apartment. He called for his partners, but they ignored him. The drug dealer then shot him in the face as he turned to flee, realizing no one was coming to help.

By some quirk of fortune, the point-blank shot didn't kill him. The bullet entered just below his eye and lodged at the top of his jaw. It did make him deaf in the left ear and left bullet fragments near his brain, causing him severe headaches for the years that followed.

As he lay in the corridor bleeding, his colleagues neglected to issue an "officer down" call—one more highly suggestive omission. It was an apartment resident who saved his life. The elderly Hispanic man called an ambulance and stayed with Serpico until a police squad car came, beating the ambulance to the scene. Serpico was taken to a hospital without being recognized by the officers who attended to him.

He was visited at the hospital by the mayor, but also on an hourly basis by police officers who attempted to make him as miserable as possible. To the sure displeasure of some, he pulled through.

When it came time for Frank Serpico to testify for the Knapp Commission, his case received immediate attention by the circumstances of the shooting. It was clear that a policeman was involved in a dangerous and even heroic assignment, one that was apparently set up as an execution for someone perceived as a stool pigeon. The public wasn't going to stand for that kind of evil behavior on the part of those trusted to protect and serve.

Before the Knapp Commission, Serpico made this statement:

Through my appearance here today . . . I hope that police officers in the future will not experience the same frustration and anxiety that I was subjected to for the past five years at the hands of my superiors because of my attempt to report corruption . . . We create an atmosphere in which the honest officer fears the dishonest officer, and not the other way around . . . The problem is that the atmosphere does not yet exist in which honest police officers can act without fear of ridicule or reprisal from fellow officers.[7]

My story may lack the intense drama of Frank Serpico's, but I recognized so many common themes. His statement before the commission resonated with me, and his frustration—the reality of honesty being punished and dishonesty rewarded—was something I had come to understand. I respected him and needed his advice.

We had several rewarding telephone conversations. I told him what I was learning about the old saying that you can't fight city hall. "I feel like I'm in a heavyweight fight with one hand tied behind my back," I said.

It was fascinating to hear the advice of someone who had fought a similar war, but in a different era. He didn't ask so many questions about the details of hazing and the Lords of Discipline. He wanted to know about my present state of mind. He expressed concern for my physical health.

Where Stefano had passionately talked about fighting dirty, Serpico quietly talked about keeping calm. These were two interlocking parts of the puzzle. I realized that Serpico's aim was true. Over time, the person with the greatest opportunity to bring me down was myself. If pressure is applied long enough, and the temperature climbs upward for long enough, something's got to give. Serpico felt that I was worrying too much about what other people might do, and not enough about my own mental, physical, and spiritual health.

"Take off your shoes," he counseled. "Walk on a soft patch of grass and remember to breathe."

I had seen Al Pacino's interpretation of him onscreen, a kind of late sixties hippie with a holster. At one time, I might have dismissed his advice as being a tad eccentric. But again, I knew I was hearing

---

7   http://www.gadflyonline.com/archive/JanFeb01/archive-serpico.html

sound advice from a friend who cared about me. Serpico had spent time recuperating in Switzerland after his ordeal. I think that the stress he lived through for so long, and the recovery he benefited from in such a contrasting atmosphere—Switzerland was for him what Hawaii was for me—changed him from the inside out. He was living to a ripe old age with a strong and positive approach to life.

I thought about how nice it would be to chill out in the Alps for a while, or spend six months in some tropic paradise. It eased my tension a little bit just to let that possible future run through my mind. It had helped to get a little push from Stefano, and it had encouraged me to get a little reassurance from Serpico.

Two friends obviously had my back, but there was also the senator, who put in a word for me from on high. But there was even a higher court of appeal. I spent a lot of time in prayer during this period. The most important friend of all was the one who I knew was watching over me, the heavenly father who has a purpose for everything and a love for everyone. It is not when life is easy, but when it's covered by crisis, that we really experience the reality of God. When we come to the end of our own resources, we turn to heaven and find out that he is there to give us inner peace and assurance.

All this input came together as a bulwark for me. Not only was I going to ride this thing out, but I was also going to enjoy getting over it someplace where I could really relax. I was feeling somewhat stronger—with a little help from my friends.

Chapter 13:

"Point Man for Every Honest Cop in America"

My friends had given me a lot to think about. Yes, I needed to take better care of my mind, body, and soul. That was the counsel of Serpico, a wise ex-cop who had walked my path. Yet I had to balance that advice with that of another friend, who wanted me to increase the pressure. If I wanted to clean up the New Jersey State Police, he said, I needed to be willing to get my hands dirty.

Okay, so I was supposed to relax while turning up the pressure? Maybe it was possible. The trick was to compartmentalize things— to go full-speed on the outside, while not letting it consume me on the inside. I had to put myself in the calm area that lies in the eye of a hurricane.

I thought about all this when an internal affairs detective gave me a call. It was time for yet another interview, another round of questions about the Lords of Discipline. They were still looking for a flaw in my story, some route for doing what they did best—burying everything in an inscrutable mass of red tape, so that the public wouldn't get too interested.

But I was prepared. I had documented everything carefully, been over all of it countless times, and my story had remained consistent. I'd gotten excellent advice from my attorney and kept my faith in God.

This interview was to occur over the phone, and I decided to fight fire with fire this time—Stefano would like that. If they could make tapes for later reference, so could I. It was legal under New Jersey law. So as the interview began, I asked the detective to hold the line for a moment and took the opportunity to set up a recording device for the phone.

There was also no law that forbade me from asking questions of my own. I knew the detective would have placed all his focus on getting certain replies from me; I wondered if he was ready to make the right replies himself. Maybe I could give my attorney something to work with.

I asked him why, after eighteen months of this investigation, the Lords of Discipline case was still not closed.

I listened carefully as he began to divulge more information than one might have expected. He admitted that there had been ongoing harassment within the State Police. This in itself was a remarkable acknowledgement, because in my observation, the state had never been willing to grant the smallest point about this practice. Yes, he said, John Oliva and I had been hazed.

Did this mean he was acknowledging the existence of the Lords of Discipline? No. That wasn't going to happen; the attorney general's office had too much invested in denial of that group.

The detective said, "Trooper Hopson, there's no doubt that you've endured some rough treatment, and that's very disturbing to all of us. I can tell you that we're taking it seriously, and our investigation of the hazing is ongoing."

I pressed the point. "Can you be specific?"

"Well, I can't really give you any details. Just know that everything is being looked into. We're taking it seriously."

I recognized, of course, the vagueness of what he offered. But I was encouraged about what I was getting on tape: the state's admission of hazing in two key instances. Without knowing it, the detective was becoming a good witness for our side.

I've mentioned the old maxim that you "can't fight city hall"— or, in this case, the state capitol. That's purported to be true because of the accumulated power that governments have. They have deep connections, inexhaustible legal resources, and an army of personnel to wear down the individual who dares to challenge them.

On the other hand, there can be exceptions. Every now and then, as everyone knows, David brings down his Goliath. Government, at certain levels, has a remarkable capacity for tripping over its own feet. Like the lumbering giant, it tends to be arrogant and overconfident. Its fatal flaw is the vast inefficiency of its own bureaucracy.

In our case, it became clear that the State Police and the attorney general's office were making more than their share of mistakes during litigation. With all its power and advantages, the government was leveling the playing field with each new development, simply by going about everything ineptly.

For example, the state withheld important documentation during the discovery process—even after a federal judge mandated them to turn over the information. After several court orders, we finally got our hands on the twelve binders packed with evidence—each the size of a metropolitan telephone directory. This is basic, elementary legal procedure. Sharing evidence is a fundamental requirement of a fair trial, and judges take it extremely seriously, severely penalizing those who violate the rules.

In addition, there were constant problems in getting state witnesses to show up for depositions. This creates incredible inconvenience, and judges will not tolerate it. In this case, the federal judge was clearly angry at the state for the simple failure to take care of business.

An op-ed piece appeared in the Newark Star-Ledger: "Release State Police Report."

The State Police were arrogant. If they hadn't been, our case never would have been necessary. Since so much was at stake, it would have been wise for them to drop the ongoing belligerence and clean up their act. Instead, they gave us advantages and opportunities we were more than willing to accept.

The long, hot summer was winding down. I knew that my private purgatory must have been coming to its own conclusion. I decided it was time for a personal outing, and I knew exactly where I wanted to go.

Through all the ups and downs of my case, I'd never forgotten about John Oliva. The sight of the fallen trooper's grieving father at the funeral home was permanently etched in my memory. So it was time to check in and see how the family was coping during these last few years. I wanted John's dad to know that I hadn't backed down from my promise to push for the abolition of hazing. At the same time, I knew that, as the pressure increased, this would help solidify my resolve. I had been through difficult enough times, but I hadn't paid with my life as John Oliva had.

The drive gave me time to think through these things, and to become angry all over again that these thoughtless predators had driven a good cop to such a tragic end. I pulled my car to the curb in front of the Oliva home, parked, and began to gather my things. I had brought a stack of news articles about our experiences—John's and mine—with the Lords of Discipline.

I walked up to the door, took a deep breath, and started to ring the bell. But the door opened first, and a familiar face was before me. "May I help you?" asked Mr. Oliva. He wasn't expecting me, and understandably enough, he didn't recognize me at first.

I smiled nervously and identified myself, and quickly gained an invitation to come in. Soon, Mrs. Oliva joined us as well. For the next several hours, we exchanged stories. I told about everything I had experienced up to this day, and the Olivas told me about their own experiences in the aftermath of their son's death. Our mutual resentment toward the Lords of Discipline bound us together.

I tried to explain what our first meeting, in the presence of John's body, had meant to me. What I wanted to convey was that, even with the profound suffering that comes with losing a child, that child did not die in vain. John Oliva's experience had galvanized me. It provided me with a rallying point, helping me to know that this stubborn persistence wasn't all about me. It was a response to a trend that had cost a family its precious son, a state its outstanding officer, and the future a leader. Such a crime could not and would not stand, and this had become real to me on the day I attended that service and met John's father. I said these things the best I could.

I concluded, "I'm going to keep up the fight, sir, no matter what it costs. It's been difficult, and I've had some low moments. But for John's sake, I'm not going to back down." Mr. Oliva listened quietly and, when I had finished, said, "Well, we appreciate that. We appreciate it more than we can say. But please, promise us you won't end up like John."

"Yes, sir, I promise," I replied. "I'm trying my best to take care of myself, and to be sure it never gets that far with me. I appreciate your concern."

I looked out the window and saw that the sun was beginning to set on a late summer evening. I was about to politely say goodbye when Mr. Oliva said, "Justin, I wonder if you'd like to visit our son's grave with us. It's not far away, and we won't stay long." I quickly replied, "It would be an honor."

We climbed into one of the cars and drove to the cemetery where John was buried. There we stood silently and regarded the grave, each of us praying or reflecting in our own way during a few moments of silence.

I studied the attractive headstone decorated with Marine Corps flags and religious iconography. I thought again about what had been stolen from the future—truly one of our best and brightest. I asked God to renew within me the spirit and resolve to do the right thing, to be endowed with the wisdom I needed, and for him to bless my efforts to keep these injustices from happening in the future.

Mr. Oliva looked over at me, and I knew it was all right to speak. "How often do you come here to visit?" I asked.

"Every day," he quietly replied.

Every day. Those words haunted me on the drive home.

Despite the sadness of its subject matter, the trip was a tonic for me. It's so easy for us to get caught up in our own problems. We need to reach out to others on a regular basis and understand the challenges that they, too, must face. There's nothing we can experience that isn't surpassed in difficulty by the lives of others we know.

Author with John Oliva

Thinking about John Oliva, and experiencing the aching cavity in his parents' lives, helped me realize that I hadn't even begun to pay the kind of price that this family had paid. Whatever I had suffered, it hadn't been brutal enough to drive me to my grave, nor had I lost a family member. As downhearted as I'd been, it couldn't approach what the surviving parents were feeling as they outlived the son they adored.

And of course, the visit also served as a powerful reminder of what my quest was all about. It wasn't to prove my personal toughness; nor was it my individual struggle against the Lords of Discipline. This was really an extension of the pledge I had taken when I received my hat and shield: *to protect and serve.* I was simply keeping my pledge, seeing that laws were enforced properly, and helping to protect future police officers from hazing and harassment.

Meanwhile, my administrative leave still had a ways to go. I settled back in for its duration with a little more patience. I began to write down a passage from time to time for cathartic purposes. In time, those passages became pages, pages became chapters, and chapters became a book. This book was born out of patience—truly a "full circle" experience for me.

I also did a much better job of using the phone to keep in touch with people I cared about, who could encourage me. I called the Olivas and followed up on our renewed friendship, and I had a few more conversations with Frank Serpico. All of these people cheered me on, and that strengthened me.

I also enjoyed crossing paths with FBI Agent Mike Narbo at a neighborhood pub in Philadelphia. Mike and I talked about our families over lunch, and we became fast friends. Mike had heard a little about my battle with the Lords of Discipline, and he was eager to find out how the situation was unfolding. I told him about the interviews, about the state's constant problems with following simple procedure, and about my own ongoing work to see that the attorney general buried the problem.

Mike was reflective as he listened to the latest developments. Then he made a statement that has stuck with me ever since. "I don't want to put too much pressure on you, Justin," he said. "But you are the point man for every honest cop in America."

It was yet another reminder of the importance of what I was doing. It was good to know there were people out there like Mike— men and women who cared as deeply about the means as they did about the ends when it came to law enforcement. In an age when integrity begins to look like the exception rather than the rule in so many corners of society, we need many thousands of people like that. I thanked him for his vote of confidence as we shook hands and parted ways.

At home, I looked out the window and saw the first colors of autumn begin to appear in the trees. There was that familiar, pleasant crispness in the air that tells you that the summer heat has done its worst, and is getting ready to take a few months off. But our case was just heating up. The Office of the Attorney General and the New Jersey State Police contacted my attorney. They were ready to talk about a settlement.

The news wasn't entirely unexpected. The internal affairs detectives had done their deeds. They had punched and probed, looking for holes, and they hadn't found any. At the end of the day, I had a solid case. From the beginning of my experience, I had the foresight to document every questionable activity I'd experienced. The evidence for hazing was indisputable, and it took a great deal of willful blindness to come to any other conclusion than one acknowledging that there was such a thing as the Lords of Discipline, and that it was an ugly cancer in New Jersey law enforcement, a nasty stain on the electric blue of the State Police.

The state may have been legally clumsy, but it wasn't stupid. Its attorneys knew there was nothing to gain by going to court and letting the story play out, so they were willing to pay out.

I had mixed emotions about that. On the one hand, it was clear that this low point of my life was finally coming to an end. One way or another, it would be resolved, and that was a profound relief. On the other hand, for me this had never been about cashing in. I was determined that a settlement shouldn't preclude an open and thorough cleaning up of the corruption that brought about this case. Surely the attorney general and internal affairs didn't want to revisit these kinds of charges over and over.

Buckman understood how I felt, and I emphasized to him that no settlement should compromise the principle that had guided us.

A settlement conference was scheduled, one where the State Police, the attorney general's office, Buckman and I would all be present in an attempt to come to terms. When the day came, I donned my best suit and my highest hopes. I wanted to come to an agreement and move on.

I sat across from the State Police Lieutenant Colonel who was second in command of the organization. He was known for his no-nonsense approach and his steely military bearing. Everyone shook hands, and the formalities were disposed of quickly. The lieutenant colonel had come prepared to award me with a commendation from the superintendent, as well as a plum administrative position at State Police headquarters. One of the selling points of the new position would be that it would assure me a soft landing in the police force, after so much tension.

That was the offer. All I had to do was drop the lawsuit, cut my losses, and forget all the bad things that had happened.

What about the Lords of Discipline? What about hazing and the corrupt culture? They were to be forgotten. The state wasn't prepared to admit they existed—there was no secret group, and there would be no reforms. If I were to accept their offer, I would, of course, be endorsing that position.

With an offer on the table, Buckman asked for a short recess. It was a formality, because we both knew what my response would be. We returned to the table and advised the lieutenant colonel that we couldn't accept such an offer.

The lieutenant colonel responded with characteristic bluntness. "I would recommend that you reconsider and accept the offer, Trooper," he said. "Otherwise, when you get back to work, I don't think you're going to like your assignment."

It was truly amazing. This man, the second in command over all our State Police, was the perfect embodiment of the wrongs we were bringing to light. He was denying the existence of hazing, then, in the same breath, threatening something that sounded suspiciously similar to it.

"Sir," I said calmly, "I didn't initiate the lawsuit for an award, and I wasn't after a cushy job at headquarters, either. Those things are not what this has been about, and I've tried to be very clear about that in every interview. If you want to make an offer that will be accepted, address the issue of reform." I paused. "Sir, may I ask you why the administration is so adamant about ignoring the culture of hazing?"

He glared at me with laser eyes as I spoke, then offered an answer that was quite visual. The lieutenant colonel quietly gathered his paperwork without speaking a word. The talking was over, I was unworthy of an honest answer, and he headed for the door.

The session had ended in a stalemate.

Chapter 14:

The Lords Go Public

According to Shakespeare's The Merchant of Venice, "The truth will out."

The truth "outed" to the tune of five thousands pages of discovery in the question of the Lords of Discipline, the New Jersey State Police's dirty little secret. This included the videotape of Krista's unlawful arrest for drunk driving, as well as interviews, certain physical evidence, and all the public records that were part of the investigation.

I remember sitting and attempting to digest the voluminous discovery materials, for hours on end. I watched the video of the events that, in a way no one could have anticipated, set all of these things into motion. I was a "fly on the wall," looking in on interviews with former colleagues who officially made their feelings known—on the record. Hopson didn't have a "trooper's mentality," according to one. He just didn't fit in, pronounced another. One veteran sergeant felt he had settled the questions of morality by popular vote: "How can forty troopers be wrong and one trooper be right?" he asked. I recognized the age-old rationalization that was meted out for nearly every kind of behavior that anyone wanted excused.

There were also a few who came short of toeing the party line. They admitted that they saw me as a stand-up guy, trying to make a difference—something they could only respect.

The Lords of Discipline affair had turned out to be the largest internal investigation in State Police history. I saw enough material and evidence to be convinced that internal affairs had acted in good faith. They had used every available resource to identify the troopers who were involved in hazing. It was all done thoroughly and sincerely.

The flaw, however, was this: State Police administration was not held accountable. I suppose it's characteristic of how the world works: Be tough on those below you in the pecking order, but don't dare lift your gaze to those levels higher than your position. Ultimately, only the administration had the power to hold itself accountable, and we knew that wasn't going to happen.

It was about a month past the ill-fated settlement conference when I received my new assignment. I was to report to the State Governmental Security Bureau, which provides security for the governor and the state employees within the capitol complex. I thought about the threat I had been given: *Accept the settlement or you won't like your assignment.* Was it going to hold true, or was it a bluff?

Frankly, I would have liked nearly anything that wasn't another week of administrative leave. By this time, I needed leave from the leave itself. I was restless to be doing something productive. But I was nervous about reporting to the capitol, and when I walked into the State Governmental Security Bureau on my first day, I felt like a round peg in a square hole. I certainly wasn't accustomed to administrative work on this scale.

Nevertheless, I threw myself into getting acquainted with the job and the people who surrounded it. I went out of my way to create positive relationships with colleagues, and focused on being a quick learner. My responsibilities were to supervise 250 state security guards, investigate criminal activity, and secure state buildings. Most of this was new to me, and of course this was more supervision than I'd yet taken on.

The great goal, as far as I was concerned, was to be evaluated on the basis of my work rather than my whistle-blower reputation. Time would tell if I was going to get my wish.

There was a commotion at the capitol complex on April 27, 2005. Several state employees reported seeing three suspicious males canvassing the area in an automobile. They were wearing masks and gave every appearance of being terrorists.

Another detective quickly joined me in investigating the call. It took only a few moments for us to identify the car containing the suspects, and we began to follow them in our patrol car. We tailed them for a short period. I then cruised to a soft stop as the suspects parked their car and began unwrapping the garments covering their faces.

With gun in hand, I quietly stepped out of the car and began to approach the men. The driver and I immediately made eye contact by way of the car's mirror. I commanded the suspects not to move. At this point, other troopers emerged, surrounding the car.

I began to question the driver, whose name turned out to be Angel, though he initially tried on several other names. As we talked, a fellow trooper reached inside the car and pulled out a Molotov cocktail, the well-known mixture of gasoline and two-cycle motor oil that is used as an incendiary device.

This was enough evidence to make an arrest. I took hold of Angel and commanded the other men to exit the car with their hands behind their heads. Restraining Angel's hands, I searched his pockets for drugs, weapons, or any other evidence of criminal activity. Angel was talking a mile a minute, assuring me that the firebomb was not his and that he had no idea how it got into his car. I suppose there was little else he could say to better his cause, once he was apprehended while wearing a mask and possessing a bomb.

After we made the arrests, we read the suspects their rights and brought them in for questioning. For hours, the suspects sat under the heat lamps while detectives questioned them concerning their motives and connections. Eventually, Angel began to give straight answers. The bomb, he said, had been earmarked for a "street" rival of his. As the details unfolded, we were able to ascertain that this was a gang-related crime, not terrorism. The state capitol, of course, was a poor choice for taking care of such business in masks. The three suspects were charged with conspiracy to commit an aggravated assault and unlawful possession of a weapon. They were jailed pending bond.

The excitement over the "terrorists"—even if they turned out to be no more than garden-variety gang members—was a rare incident. At the State Governmental Security Bureau, life and work were fairly placid. I was less likely to be involved in the kind of shenanigans that had gotten me knee-deep in tension during patrol duties. On the other hand, working in administration created its own problems, particularly of the bureaucratic sort. I found out that the guards themselves could pose greater security problems than the people or places they were guarding.

To this day, I'm baffled by how difficult it is to suspend or fire a state employee. In the private sector, of course, those who don't do their jobs quickly find themselves looking for other work. This is not always true in state government. Take the case of a security guard I knew who actually left his post. He taped a note to his guard post that said, "Will be back," and headed off to do something else. The "something else," as it turned out, was the purchase of illegal drugs. The 250-pound man, neatly decked out in his security guard uniform, passed out on a park bench.

We received word of this from the paramedics who whisked him off to the hospital. "We've got one of your guards," they said. "He took too many drugs." The uniform and state-issued radio had made him easy to trace.

You might think a security guard who bought and used illegal drugs while on duty would be immediately terminated—or at the very least, indefinitely suspended. However, we're talking about state employment. My unit conducted an investigation and moved to suspend or fire the man. The local union got involved, and then the attorney general's office. Their request was for no criminal charges or termination. Rather, the verdict was a round of counseling and a few weeks off.

I could also tell the story of Nyla, a thirty-year-old guard with a hardcore habit of tardiness. Not only did Nyla tend to show up late, she often fell asleep at her post. A bit of observation indicated to me that she was dealing with personal issues, so I tried to be a little lenient and help her do better. The problem was that she turned up on the wrong end of a narcotics sting operation. She was arrested for purchasing crack cocaine and twenty-five grams of marijuana in the middle of a neighborhood known for its drug traffic.

I confronted Nyla, asking how a trusted security guard could let this happen in her life. She gave me a desperate tale about how her son had slipped the drugs into her purse for safekeeping. The police, she claimed, had conducted a random search and stumbled upon the crack and the weed her son had planted. The story was farfetched. Even so, the verdict was counseling and a more convenient work schedule.

At times, I couldn't help but consider how the government was spending its taxpayers' money. Yet again, my supervisor arrested one of our security guards for possession of marijuana. The man was working and securing state property, but it so happened that he was carrying a bag of weed in his pocket as he went about his duties. I suppose it was there for his downtime. The verdict handed down by the administration was a week suspension, and reassignment to a new guard post.

As these events began to add up, I put in a formal suggestion to institute a drug-screening program for security personnel to the State Police, the local union, and the attorney general's office. I was frankly surprised that such a thing wasn't already in place. After all, don't we want to take every possible precaution to know that the men and women who are securing our state buildings and personnel are cognitive to do so?

I did my homework, looking into the legalities, methods, and expenses for such a program. I envisioned testing for marijuana, heroin, barbiturates, methamphetamine, and opiates through hair follicle drug testing. Some might wonder why we would test hair rather than urine. The difference is one of time span: urine tests are useful for detecting drug use during the last twenty-four to forty-eight hours, but hair (at sufficient length) can indicate drug use during a period stretching as far as three months.

I learned the basics of this practice and put together a written proposal for pre-employment drug screening of security guards, as well as random drug testing for the duration of employment. I felt I was bringing a solid suggestion to the table, strengthening our security measures and preventing drug-related issues.

But by now, you may have guessed where I'm going with this—I was informed, "off the record," that the program wouldn't be practical. Why? Because if the state were to immediately begin testing for drugs, it could stand to lose up to forty percent of its trained guard force.

The official reason, of course, was more technical: "reasons of liability." But how much sense did that make? Liability, if we stop and think about it, is a powerful reason for, not against, drug testing.

In the fall of 2005, I accompanied my attorney to a hearing at a federal courthouse in Camden. The subject was this: Could the state classify its report on hazing and evidence of the Lords of Discipline? I had refused to agree to a settlement requiring me to keep my mouth shut and let them bury the report. I believe that governmental reports and investigations belong to the taxpayers who have funded them. In a democracy built around the idea of freedom, we have a right to open records—to seeing what we've paid for, and having access to the information about how our governmental agencies are serving us.

Leading up to the hearing, the State Police and attorney general's office had used a "lie and deny" campaign on issues pertaining to the Lords. Their stance was that, sure—a little hazing went on here and there. When found, they asserted, it was dealt with accordingly. But there was no organized, ongoing *program* of hazing or intimidation. And "there was no group of troopers known as the Lords of Discipline," as a spokesman for the Division of Criminal Justice insisted.

We felt we could demonstrate otherwise, but to do so, we needed access to the state's own findings. This hearing would determine whether the state had the right to withhold them from the public.

As the hearing began, the state made its case. Confidentiality, the attorneys argued, must be protected. These were tense matters, and people wouldn't come forward to speak out in the future if they didn't believe they could do so under the protective cloak of secrecy. This is the classic strategy for keeping embarrassing information out of the light of day.

I watched as my attorney, Bill Buckman, performed his quiet magic. He presented a smooth argument on behalf of the people, the taxpayers. They have a right to know how their police conduct themselves, he pointed out. As Bill made his case, my eyes traversed the perimeter of the courtroom, where reporters were making careful notes—the more of those I felt, the better for our side. The public always tends to be in favor of having access to the truth.

It went well. The judge listened noncommittally, then gave the State Police ten days to provide their report to the public. Then we rose with him and watched him retreat to his chambers. I let out a long breath.

Outside the courtroom, several reporters asked for our comments on the ruling. Buckman said, "I requested thousands of pages of raw data from the investigation, and now I want the report to be made public. They are trying to engage in spin control over a very troubled investigation, with very troubled conclusions, which they don't even want people to scrutinize."

It felt strange to be part of one of these lawyer-on-the-steps moments that I had seen so many times on news shows and even in movies.

After the reporters were gone and we were walking to our cars, Buckman told me, "Well, things are going in our favor. That was fun."

Always content to let a good attorney do the talking, I simply smiled. I wasn't certain I would describe any of this as "fun," exactly, but it was definitely good to be on the side in whose favor the judge ruled. And I knew that the state wasn't having fun at all right now. Their efforts to hide the Lords of Discipline had failed. The group was out in the light, and now the public would become aware.

Could it really be that a difference would finally be made?

Right on deadline and as ordered, the state issued its report. Naturally, it was heavily redacted, meaning that the names of accused Lords, high-ranking officials, and a confidential informant were withheld.

A number of highlights were contained in the report, which ran to fifty-two pages. For example, the public was able to read about a list of rules and regulations signed by the Lords and posted on troopers' lockers. The state said it had interviewed more than 250 members of the State Police during a two-year period. These witnesses had spoken of being sexually harassed, physically assaulted, and relentlessly ridiculed. Incidents extending as far back as the nineteen-seventies were covered. Dozens of troopers were known to have worn or owned tee shirts boasting of their affiliation with the group.

News reporters, of course, quickly gravitated toward what they felt were the "juicy" parts—actual incidents that could be described to their viewers or readers. They also wanted to know why strong leads from a confidential informant weren't pursued. Many citizens, for the first time, began to learn about the difficult lives of female troopers, who were constantly confronted with derogatory pictures, poems, and fliers, and ridiculing perceived sexual orientation or physical appearance. These actions wouldn't be tolerated in any ordinary workplace, but they were a common part of police culture.

The plight of black troopers also came to light. African Americans endured name-calling and second-class treatment. On at least one occasion, a trooper had watermelon placed in his locker. These things were happening at the beginning of the twenty-first century, not the twentieth century.

Then, of course, my own story was detailed. It was clear that I had been targeted simply for refusing to participate in an unlawful arrest and false report. I had been punished for upholding my oath.

The report stated that seven troopers had been disciplined, and that the state had settled harassment lawsuits to the tune of $650,000—funds that came, again, from hard-working taxpayers. How were they going to feel about that use of their money? [8]

So what had the state learned from all this? It was stated clearly near the beginning of their report: "There are no visible connections

---

8   April 25, 2006, *The Trentonian*

between the accused harassers. It appears that each incident is separate and arises out of situations that are unique from one another."

In other words, forget the dozens of troopers walking around in clearly legible tee shirts. Don't worry about the "rules and regulations" signed by the Lords, and posted on lockers, or the accounts of scores of troopers who knew all about the group, what it did, and who was in it. There *were* no Lords of Discipline, just an ongoing series of unfortunate events with no particular pattern to connect them.

The State of New Jersey held up a large picture with a clear pattern of numbered dots—but refused to admit they could be connected to form a picture.

The senator I'd previously contacted—the one who compared the Lords to an "SS within the police force"—wrote a follow-up letter to the attorney general and, this time, to the senate judiciary committee, demanding a wider and fuller review of the report and its findings. "Although the report may not have identified a formal dues-paying organization that is called the Lords of Discipline," he said, "the report fails to inspire public confidence."

He continued,

The sheer number of reprimands and the large settlements seem to indicate that some form of organized retaliatory harassment took place. More importantly, it appears that all of the culpable troopers have remained on the force. Because the State Police have retained a suspect group of individuals who have demonstrated a propensity for rogue behavior, the risk of harm to troopers like Justin Hopson remains.[9]

And with that, the bureaucracy simply battened down the hatches, as it had always done, and hoped the storm wouldn't last too long. It feebly held out the promise of "sensitivity training" that

---

9   April 29, 2006, *The Philadelphia Inquirer*

it would institute for its troopers, and, above all, banked its hopes upon the short memory of the public. Just get through a couple of ugly news cycles, and once again the State Police could avoid the unspeakable task of instituting genuine reform.

More charges, more investigations, and more huge cash settlements would surely lie in the future. But tough reform? Not so much.

My objective was simply to make it through the lawsuit, doing everything I could to hold out for the possibility of seeing the State Police clean itself up. Ultimately, I knew there was only so much I could do.

What I could accomplish was to take care of myself. On days off, I drove to the beach and watched the waves roll onto the sand, breathing in the ocean air and letting the stress uncoil itself from my mind. Nature is good medicine. I walked along the beach and thought about Serpico's advice. He wanted me to feel the grass between my toes, but I figured he would approve of sand under the soles of my feet instead.

I thought about all my efforts to get something good done, and to protect my own mind and body as well. In situations like this one, we come to a point of realizing our limitations, then (if we're wise) clearing our minds and handing the rest over to God. I think that's the ultimate secret to navigating the hard rapids of anxiety— knowing that some things are best left in his perfect hands, and being satisfied we've personally done our best.

I know God cares deeply about our integrity, and I felt I could stand before him, at the end of this life, and say that I had done what I could and hopefully live up to the standards he desires for us. There had been many nights when I couldn't sleep, but now they might be behind me. If I had given in to the dishonest practices that had been demanded of me, I would have carried the guilt through the rest of my life. Better to lose a little rest now than a great of deal of it later.

I decided that this is what life is about for me. I want all my involvements to be rooted in a solid core of integrity, so that people know I am trustworthy on every front. I define integrity as incorruptibility, the refusal to swerve from a clearly defined standard of conduct.

But isn't this what defines life for all of us? How many little tests do we face every day? A typical job holds thousands of opportunities to cut corners, to take what isn't ours, to avoid work or responsibilities that is required, or to falsify documents. At home, we face the temptation to cheat on income tax, while society says, "Don't worry, everybody does it." That's an ominous sign for our future.

Integrity is at issue everywhere we look. Our politicians, our business leaders, and our religious leaders often remind us that trust is hard won and easily forfeited. My lifetime seems to be defined as a series of national scandals: Watergate in 1974, Abscam in 1980, Iran-Contra in 1986, even a president lying under oath in the nineties.

In the business world, we've lived through Enron, WorldCom, and insider trading on Wall Street. It seems we can't trust our banks and lending institutions with our retirement funds. America is presently reeling from a financial recession that might largely have been avoided if the key players had followed the simple path of honesty, as well as sound trading and lending practices.

We turn to professional sports and find that even in games, athletes are cheating to get a competitive edge through chemical enhancements. Meanwhile, many of the authors and journalists who have covered these events have been caught plagiarizing. No matter what we do or what we seek, the issue always comes down to integrity.

The message we seem to hear throughout our culture is *just succeed, whatever you have to do to make it happen.* It was a viewpoint reflected by the character of Gordon Gekko in the movie *Wall Street,* who said, "Greed is good."

I would think that the events of the last couple of years have shown that it's never good. In the end, it destroys our world.

The stability of civilization depends upon the establishment of order and integrity. To the extent that we treat each other with deference and honesty, we help each other toward better, more secure and happy lives. But to the extent we begin taking care of ourselves at the complete expense of others, stealing from, lying to, and cheating everyone else, it all begins to fall apart. The world becomes a dark and primitive place then. At this primary level of social interaction, we install law enforcement officers to protect and serve us. We have had them, in different forms, as long as there has been advanced human civilization.

What happens, then, when we know that those uniformed officers are no more trustworthy than anyone else? Is it really such a big deal if they, too, cut a few corners—say, using racially profiling to save time, because they're sure certain kinds of people are more likely to be guilty? Or harassing new officers who happen to be women, because the group thinks they won't fit in with "the boys"? What about expediting an arrest, when some of the details aren't in place, by bending a few facts on the report?

Some would say, "Hey, that's inevitable. I know my police have the right goals, and I guess the end justifies the means."

I don't believe that. I do think that our law enforcement personnel should maintain the highest possible standards. We need to possess full assurance that they can be fully trusted for our protection. I'm deeply saddened when I read about the LA Police and its Rampart CRASH Unit scandal, in which several officers participated in gross misconduct and cost the LAPD $125 million to settle 140 lawsuits. I'm troubled to learn of the NYPD Ticket-Fixing scandal, in which sixteen officers fixed hundreds of traffic tickets costing New York City up to $2 million in lost revenue.

In my own state there was Operation Slap Shot, an investigation that uncovered a multimillion-dollar sports gambling ring, financed by NHL Coach Rick Tocchet and run by a New Jersey State Trooper. My colleague was arrested, indicted, and later fired for his involvement in the gambling ring. At the time, he had hundreds of thousands of dollars in the bank, $250,000 worth of Rolex watches, and nine plasma-screen televisions seized from his home.

In all these cases, police officers abuse their position. They prey rather than protect, and serve themselves rather than society. Before they can police our world, officers must police themselves. It's not easy to stand up against peer pressure and the danger of recrimination, but it must be done. For too long we have excused certain things by holding that there are "gray areas." When it comes to law enforcement, there are no gray areas. This is why there are times, unfortunately, when guilty criminals are released on so-called "technicalities."

We don't like to see it happen, but officers of the law can't hold to search-and-seizure requirements only when it's convenient. They can't read Miranda rights just if they happen to think of it. These are our civil rights, they exist for our protection, and therefore they're sacred. The price of that is that we hold our officers, and all their practice, to the highest possible standards. The more we do that, the more stable and safe our streets and neighborhoods will be.

Serpico said it best: "Dishonest cops should be made to fear honest cops, and not the other way around."

I thought about all of this as I walked along a quiet beach and heard the cries of sea gulls. I know I can live with myself. I will sleep well at night, and that will extend from now until the day I leave this life. That path had to be chosen when I was a raw rookie, only eleven days into my service. It cost more than a few sleepless nights up front, but that's the path I chose.

I like to think that my actions made some small difference; time will tell. I know that a man like Serpico, with the wide reach of his story, made a great deal of difference in the standards eventually required of New York City cops.

And finally, I think about public servants of all kinds, now and in the future—perhaps reading this book. Are you willing to blow the whistle? If it comes down to it, will you insist on integrity, and report dishonest or predatory behavior?

I advise you to be courageous. For one thing, the future depends upon the decisions made on ordinary highways, or in ordinary workplaces, by ordinary individuals like you and me. You must decide whether you will leave your field of service in better condition than you found it, or you will perpetuate things that shouldn't be happening. For now, you may feel anxious. But what about five years from now? Ten? Thirty?

Never underestimate the importance of an unburdened conscience. I always kept in mind the phrase, "A clean conscience makes a soft pillow." So my mind was clear and the future finally seemed promising. But life had one more great twist in store for me.

Chapter 15:

Out of the Blue

Life is always evaluated on the far side of its events. We progress through its various seasons, and then make sense of what has transpired. We tend to divide our experiences into neat chapters of our lives. We call these chapters childhood, education, this job, the next job, marriage, parenthood, and so on. From womb to tomb, we live now and organize in retrospect, as we pass identifiable hurdles.

So life becomes a story, and each person sees himself or herself as the hero. The problem comes when we realize we're not fully in control of the narrative. Just as we're under the impression that we've defeated some giant, or survived some storm—something else comes out of nowhere and knocks us down. It's the beginning of another chapter, and as usual, we never saw it coming.

The plot twist in my own story came just as I was sure that there couldn't be another ounce of drama left to emerge.

The new chapter began on the morning of March 13, 2006. The day began unremarkably at five o'clock, as the alarm clanged its abrasive end to my slumber. I attended to the usual morning rituals, packing a lunch, checking my firearm carefully, and grabbing a minimal breakfast to eat on the run.

I turned on the radio as I settled into the patrol car in my driveway. A dispatcher was doling out the usual police jargon. There were no emergencies; all was calm on our front.

I pushed the dial to a weather report to find out what conditions I'd be dealing with for the day. We were in store for an unseasonably warm and sunny mid-March afternoon. I looked over my shoulder and backed the car down the drive, mulling over the eight-hour shift that lay in front of me. It should be a pleasant day, after which I'd be ready to go jogging with a good friend, as planned. Life had settled into a calm routine, and I had no complaints about that.

The morning brought a minor theft. I duly investigated it and filled out the necessary reports. Beyond that, nothing of consequence happened. My shift reached its end, and I handed in the patrol log documenting a fairly uneventful day. A few of us exchanged a pleasantry or two before I said goodbye and headed for the parking lot and home.

I was looking forward to enjoying the nice weather and working up a good sweat during my jog. As I pulled the patrol car onto the interstate, I hoped I wouldn't see any activity requiring me to pull someone over and write a ticket. *All you drivers please behave,* I thought. *You don't want to receive the citation, and I don't want to give it to you.*

The appearance of my car, of course, made things easier. Other vehicles peeled to the right lane as soon as they spotted its markings. I finally took an exit by way of a curved concrete ramp and came to a stop at a traffic light there. As I waited for red to become green, another car pulled up beside me, its radio blaring with the windows down. A young couple sat in the front seat, and they regarded me curiously. I was accustomed to the speculative stares that all men or women in uniform receive.

As the light turned green, my drive continued. I was approaching fifty miles per hour when I noticed a black car pull out of a shopping center and onto the highway. With no other cars in front of mine, I kept a straight course. But the black car suddenly cut me off, causing me to slam on my brakes and veer toward an escape lane. It was too late. The impact came before my instincts could kick in and let me brace my defenses. My ears were filled by the brief yet awful cacophony that is the mingling of twisting steel, shattering glass, and scraping rubber.

The din subsided, and the pain rushed in.

I felt a pang behind my head that told me I'd sustained whiplash. My vision was blurred. The last thing I could remember was the black car; my sights had been locked in on its erratic movement. The vehicle had spun out of control when the front of my patrol car struck it, causing the black car's trunk to implode.

Shattered glass had exploded into the open side windows of my car. Though I'd clamped my eyes shut to avoid the deadly shards, the left side of my face had been exposed. The car had come to a full halt, and so, it seemed, had time.

I was fully conscious; I had that going for me. Driven by the super-powered rush of adrenaline that life provides in such situations, I threw open the door of my car, both to escape and to check on the other party in the collision. That was the simple instinct of a trained state trooper who was accustomed to highway calamities, even if he wasn't used to being at the focal point of them.

A quick glance told me that the black car had driven its last mile. It was totaled, and I had grave concerns about its driver. As I rushed toward the car's doors and windows, I was infuriated by the traffic around me. Though none of us like "rubber-neckers," there is something worse, and that is the prospect of cars hurrying by, driving over pieces of bumper and broken glass. Initial witnesses simply want to get away from the scene and any involvement in it. I needed them to stay clear so I could get to the other driver as quickly as possible—his or her life might well have hung in the balance.

Upon getting there, I found two Asian men who were clearly in full shock mode. I was overjoyed to see they were both wearing seatbelts and bore no visible injuries. "Are you all right?" I shouted at the driver.

He nodded slowly, and I could just make out a faint "yes."

Then I inspected the passenger and asked him the same question. He acknowledged that he was in good shape from a physical standpoint.

"You two please stay in the car," I said. "Sit tight while I call for an ambulance."

As I walked back to my battered patrol car, I felt tremendous relief that the other two men had come through all right. It was becoming obvious by the minute that they were much more fortunate than me. I was sore and bleeding, and my neck was screaming at me. I gingerly climbed behind the wheel again and called in the accident to my supervisor. Then I sat back and waited for help to come.

Keeping still, of course, only accentuated the discomfort. My back was beginning to freeze up as a burning sensation was working its way down my leg. Then a cold sweat began to come over me, and it became very difficult to breathe.

I was happy to see a couple of responding officers and an ambulance.

The two police officers were trying to coax me onto the stretcher and into the EMS. One look had shown them that I was in obvious need of care. But I was stubborn. Injured though I was, I had a double role on this scene. I was not only a victim but also the officer in charge, because I had witnessed it all firsthand. I refused to leave the scene of the accident. That may seem a bit legalistic, but I had become extremely cautious about my position in regard to the State Police. Something like this could provide them, right out of the blue, with an opportunity to make some interpretation that left me at fault, whether I was injured or not. I would just have to handle the stabbing pain.

As the moments passed, the feeling in my back grew nearly intolerable. I sat in my seat, the same seat I'd climbed into that morning in such a comfortable and carefree way, and actually watched a lump of bird droppings splatter on the windshield before me. *Great,* I thought. *What a lucky day, on so many levels.*

Soon another official vehicle pulled up, with its siren revolving. A State Police sergeant stepped out of the car and began his inspection of the accident. I gave him a full statement of what had happened with the two vehicles. My car was in much better shape than the other, though the black car had certainly done a better job of protecting its occupants. I drove myself to the local hospital in the patrol car.

They X-rayed me head to toe, and gave me a CAT-scan as well. After surveying all the damage I'd sustained, the doctor referred me to an orthopedic surgeon.

The days that followed are best forgotten. They were filled with pain in many parts of my body. I felt paralyzed in the lower back, and that alone was enough to keep me confined to bed rest. As I pushed myself to get well, life presented so many little frustrations—things we tend to take for granted. Simply sitting and tying my shoes was an experiment in stabbing pain. An ordinary sneeze might send me to my knees in excruciating spasms.

It's true that we don't value precious things until we lose them. As a young man accustomed to prime fitness, I realized just how little I had valued the blessings of physical health. The body is a complex, harmonious undertaking of countless muscles, ligaments, and bones. They work together so seamlessly that we never realize what walking, living, breathing miracles we are until we lose the ability of simple movement—hopefully for just a while.

I had been on my way to go jogging that day. Jogging! I could barely sit in or rise from a chair now. I did what we all do in such situations: I swore to myself that, when I got well, I'd more fully appreciate what it means to be whole.

But what about the other thing? Something else was being stripped away from me, too, and in this case it wasn't going to come back. My career as a New Jersey State Trooper was at an end, because of the seriousness of the accident. The fitness requirements for a trooper are quite demanding. Completing the annual 1.5 mile run in thirteen minutes or less would now be much more difficult, and even eking out thirty-two pushups and thirty-four sit-ups seemed out of the question for me. Trying to pass the sit-and-reach flexibility test with a tangled back seemed counterintuitive to me.

I'd be healthy again, but I would patrol no more. I'd protect and serve no longer, at least officially. How much was I going to miss the life?

Life is a rich pageant of irony. Things happen to us that would seem trite if we placed them into a novel or a movie. Yet here, in the real world, events take on such strange symmetry.

For me the irony was this: I had fought for so many months for the simple, ordinary life of an officer of the law. I had my moments of wondering about the possibilities of other lines of work, occupations with lower stress and higher pay. My dream job had often felt more like a nightmare. Yet it was the career I had chosen, and if I ever left it, I would leave it on my terms—not because I was intimidated or forced out by the pressure of others. My fight had been with flesh and blood, starting with a single supervisor, then a group in a barracks, and finally a state bureaucracy. I had stood up against some formidable forces, and none of them had succeeded in knocking me down.

But where men had failed, the forces of nature had prevailed. After months of physical therapy, chiropractic adjustments, epidural injections, and pain meds, I raised the white flag. I'd had enough. I finally listened to one of my treating physicians who said, "Justin, your back will only get worse." The ruptured disk in my back and the radiculopathy in my right leg took away my capacity for law enforcement. One routine drive, one trip home, had done what the accumulated power of the machine could not—gotten me out of the State Police.

Dealing with courts and lawyers, we have at least some degree of control. We make decisions and prepare ourselves to live with them. But in the flicker of an eyelash, when some unforeseen calamity befalls us, we know we had no say in the matter. It just happened—it could have been the next guy just as easily! We spend time recuperating, reliving the events, thinking, "If only I had left five minutes later, or if only I had gone home by another way." But at the end of the day, we know that things simply happen; we can't control them, though we can, in fact, control our responses to them.

Therefore it was frustrating to lose my career in one swift blow, especially since I had given so much of myself to protect it. Then again, I had conflicting emotions about this development. Every dark cloud has a silver lining.

For example, no one could ever say I had quit. But it was liberating to have the decision made so incredibly simple. If the state had continued turning up the heat, harassing me in various ways, I couldn't have held out forever. It was going to grow more than tiresome, having to look over my shoulder whenever I was around other troopers. But the longer I went, the harder it would have been to quit. That decision would have taken a long, agonizing period of time.

Now I would never have to make it at all; life had done it for me. I don't believe God sits in heaven and sets up traffic collisions, but I do believe he uses everything that transpires in life, good or bad. In Romans 8:28, St. Paul writes that all things work together for the good of those who know God and are called according to his purposes. I believed God was using this new twist of fate to send my life in a fresh direction, and perhaps one that would take advantage of the skills and wisdom I'd gained through the ordeals of my past.

We can't change the past, but we can use it. What could I do with mine?

At first, I was skeptical. I brooded a little bit over what was lost, and thought, *I'll never again feel the exhilaration, the sheer adrenaline charge, of investigating a crime. What other line of work could offer that?*

And this thought suddenly brought a new one to the fore. As I thought about investigating crime, Detective Everson and the 1979 cold case leaped into my mind. That was it! When I had done those interviews and led that investigation, I had never felt so motivated, so fulfilled by my work. Wasn't it possible to use the principles of investigation without being an officer of the law? Weren't there, in fact, detectives who were self-employed—who used all their skills, all their passion for justice, without the elements of barracks room politics?

Private investigators.

I felt the chill of excitement as I began to think and plan toward a new career. As I considered the possibility of becoming a private investigator, I realized just how perfectly my initial career had prepared me for this possible new one. I had learned so much about my strengths and weaknesses, about other people, about the law—and I had picked up a great deal of practical wisdom from Detective Everson.

I couldn't have planned it any better—right down to the day. March 13th, the date of the accident, fell four years to the date after I had opposed the unlawful arrest and began the long skid that was my career as a State Trooper. Too neat, too trite for a movie. Again, I had to look toward the heavens and say, *Is that you, God? Am I the recipient of divine intervention?* It was odd—I had spent so many months agonizing over the Lords of Discipline; maybe I was learning something about the discipline of the Lord. Whatever one may believe about things, we can all agree that there comes a time of deciding to make the best of a bad situation. I happened to believe that God was guiding me in that, and it gave me a positive and confident attitude.

As a token of my new and more carefree life, I found myself a friend to accompany me on the journey. Murphy was a one-year-old English Bulldog, the runt of his litter. He came from a home that could no longer care for him. I was delighted to provide him a new one. Maybe I identified with the stubbornness of a bulldog.

I didn't identify with his drool problem, to be honest. Not only that, but Murphy had flatulence issues capable of quickly clearing any room. I needed no detective skills to suspect this was one of the *real* reasons his previous family was so willing to dispense with him.

He smelled, he drooled, and he had that sad face characteristic of his breed—the face of a ninety-year-old man on the body of a compact marine. Murphy was a strange choice of companions for such a time, yet no one could have made me smile so often. Sometimes I broke out laughing just because he walked into the room. A dog is truly a friend like no other. Murphy was pain therapy that wasn't available in any bottle.

Chapter 16:

Unfinished Business

Have you ever tried walking away from your life's passion? I found that you can take the man out of the police, but you can't easily take the police out of the man.

Our history defines us as human beings. We talk about living in the present and leaving the past behind; we see ourselves severing ties and moving neatly from one job or one relationship. What we find is that we've been so profoundly shaped by our experiences that they go with us into everything we do.

Sure, people told me to get the Lords of Discipline out of my system. They cared about me and felt I'd be healthier and happier if I could take that burden off my shoulders, leave it somewhere in the wreckage of the accident that ended my law enforcement career, and simply move on.

Cleaning up the New Jersey State Police had simply become too deep a passion for me. I was caught up in a period of creating a new life, but there was unfinished business I could not abandon. I knew that if I dropped my efforts to stimulate law enforcement reform, then it could truly be said that my experiences had served no service to the citizenry. The state was banking on public forgetfulness, hoping I would take the settlement they offered, and then simply go away and shut up.

Therefore, I kept up my pressure to get reform into legislation. I put together a proposal to establish the State of New Jersey Anti-Hazing Law. It would apply to hazing in many places not simply in the police realm, but also in the workplace and beyond. I wanted my experience to set a new precedent for eliminating the dangerous and unethical practices of intimidation that are rampant in so many institutions. There would be a zero- tolerance policy, including termination for any government employee found guilty of hazing or harassing a colleague.

The proposal offered a careful definition of what constituted hazing, and there were also clear parameters for how it should be punished. One of the critical points of the policy was to offer full protection to those who came forward to report misconduct. The greatest challenge in prosecuting certain crimes is the reluctance of people to admit they've been victimized. They have to know they can safely step out of the shadows to deliver their information without any negative ramifications.

I attempted to deal with all of these issues in the careful proposal for an anti-hazing law for the State of New Jersey. I scheduled a meeting with Gerard Duffy, a member of the judiciary committee, to discuss the document. This was the first step in what I knew would be a long and complex process; I had no illusions about the machinery of legislation, and how difficult it is to push through new laws.

I also contacted the National Whistleblower Center in Washington, DC. Since 1988, the center has served the public as a nonprofit, nonpartisan, tax-exempt, educational advocacy organization dedicated to helping whistleblowers. It works closely with citizens who have been bold enough to expose unacceptable practices in many fields, including government work. For example, the NWC led a successful six-year campaign to reform the FBI's Forensic Crime Lab, leading to reviews of misconduct in crime labs nationwide. Wrongful convictions have been overturned in any number of cases, and falsely convicted and imprisoned citizens have gained their freedom. The center has an attorney referral service to help whistleblowers have access to skilled legal representation, and there are also public education programs.

Another example is the case of Dr. Jonathan Fishbein, who exposed unethical and improper medical problems within the National Institutes of Health's drug safety clinical trials program. The Center's successful sponsorship of Dr. Fishbein's work led to sweeping reforms by the United States Department of Health and Human Services, and there were new provisions of protection for whistleblowers that came forward.

I contacted the National Whistleblower Center and acquainted it with the saga of the Lords of Discipline. The Center then wrote a supportive letter to the Senate Judiciary Chairman on my behalf. I knew that a few words from this national organization would carry a certain amount of clout. I was also sending a message that I would do everything in my power to make police hazing a national issue not just a local one.

Furthermore, I found a woman named Dr. Susan Lipkins, who was a national expert in the realm of hazing. Dr. Lipkins has focused a great deal of her attention on high school and college hazing and violence, which make up the more common and well-publicized national problems. But she's also worked against this trend in other contexts, such as hazing in the military and in law enforcement. She's been an advocate with a national voice, appearing on *Oprah, Larry King Live, The Today Show, The O'Reilly Factor, Good Morning America, CBS News, Inside Edition,* and countless other radio and television shows and networks. Dr. Lipkins listened with interest to my experience, and offered helpful guidance in drafting a state anti-hazing law.

Currently, the state law 2C: 40-3 is in place to address hazing and aggravated hazing within New Jersey's institutions of higher education. The law states that hazing is a disorderly person's offense, but is specifically intended for student and fraternal organizations. No such state law is in place to prohibit hazing in the workplace, so I proposed to expand the 2C: 40-3 law to statewide agencies. Why? Because based on my experience, some adults still act like unruly frat boys.

I now felt I had done my homework, gotten good advice, and gotten some powerful and far-reaching support in my corner. The heat was being turned up; surely the state legislature would begin to feel the pressure to establish a law against hazing. After all, why should such a practice be protected?

I was ready to see movement toward the new legislation. But time began to pass. Soon my phone calls to the judiciary weren't being returned, and my e-mails were being ignored. What happened to the New Jersey Anti-Hazing Law?

It suffered the fate of thousands of good ideas; our reform initiative became lost in the deep abyss of state governmental foot-dragging. Squeakier wheels got the grease, I suppose. Our proposal, I'm told, was never seriously considered.

It was easy to be discouraged and frustrated. I tried to keep in mind the wise words of Booker T. Washington: "Success is to be measured not so much by the position that one has reached in life as by the obstacles which he has overcome while trying to succeed."

As I tied up the loose ends of my career with the State Police, I decided not to let this cause fade away. Writing this book is one way of getting the word out. If enough people know the facts and if they are willing to speak out we can get it done. We simply need a passion on our side that exceeds the apathy on the government side.

In 2007, my retirement from the New Jersey State Police became official. The moment came when I handed over my gun and badge before attending the exit interview. There's no way not to feel the gravity of the moment, the symbolism of surrendering those two basic symbols of the public trust. As an officer, they've been an extension of your body, the primary symbols of your very identity; once you give them back, you've truly stepped back into the ranks of ordinary citizenry. I reaffirmed to myself that the standards of discipline and integrity from this career would carry over into my future work. I may not wear the crisp blue uniform, but I would continue to honor the things that it symbolized—and to fight the things it should never accompany.

The exit interview is an administrative function. We discussed my police pension and my attendance at the annual retirement ceremony. I smiled when the latter subject was broached, and respectfully declined the invitation. To me, that function was for the fine officers who had served for many more years than me. I'd had a short, if truly eventful career. It was time for me to move on, to find new work and become immersed in it.

I felt a surge of emotion as I climbed into my car for the final drive home. I may no longer be on the State Police payroll, but I had work still to do—unfinished business. I thought back over the five tense years since my badge was presented to me: good moments, plenty of negative ones, and most of all, life lessons. I was humbled by the wisdom that had come to me in such a short period. Most true wisdom comes the hard way, through difficulty rather than comfort. If learning comes through problems, I should have a PhD by now.

I looked at my hands on the steering wheel and briefly loosened them. *Don't hold on so tight all the time, I thought.* Loosen up. *Let go and let God.* Everything, after all, is in his hands. If I really believe that is true, then I don't need to be constantly anxious.

Soon my house was on the market, and I was drawing up plans to relocate. That was a big step for me, because New Jersey had always been my home. But in my heart, I knew it was time to make a clean break with the past. I knew it was time to make a clean break with the past. New Jersey and I simply had too much history together. Psychologically, it would feel liberating to start afresh in a brand-new locale. In the back of my mind, it also seemed prudent to put a few miles between some resentful state troopers and myself. I knew how some of them looked at me, and I knew the Lords of Discipline had no particular reason to disband—not while the state wouldn't even admit their existence. It wasn't a bad idea to put a few extra highway miles between us.

I realized I didn't even need to wait for my house to sell. The market was poor, and it could take a year or more to make the sale. I couldn't imagine waiting that long without new and engrossing work. It would be "house arrest" all over again. So I packed my bags, loaded the truck, and made the rounds to say goodbye to those I loved. I don't really enjoy those awkward moments of saying goodbye. Yet I realized as I did so that I had a number of really good friends, and that's one way to measure a successful life. Was I making a mistake? What if I failed to reinvent myself in some new part of the country, and what if I had trouble establishing new relationships?

I looked at several options in the sunny South, a region that made a lot of sense for my future. Finally I settled on Charleston, South Carolina, a city that has a little of everything going for it. Hitting Interstate 95 for the long drive southward provided another symbolic moment for me. I drove seven hundred miles and made my way to what was once known as "Charles Towne," a city with such a wealth of history. Coming into town, I admired the famous skyline with its old steeples and hallowed avenues. There was the Battery, looking across the bay to Fort Sumter, where the Civil War officially began. Art, culture, and Southern charm were everywhere. I was going to like it here.

I was excited about renting the bottom floor of an antebellum home in downtown Charleston, in the heart of the historic district, and soon I was part of the flow—shrimp and grits, sweet tea, and a slower pace.

There was a bit of irony implicit in this move, too. Nearby was The Citadel, the military academy that inspired former cadet Pat

Conroy to write the novel *The Lords of Discipline*. I certainly hadn't thought of that when I chose Charleston as my destination. Now I could only smile at the poetic justice of moving from the site of the "real" Lords of Discipline to the home of the fictional ones. Someday, I hoped there would be nothing left but the fiction.

On the third day of October 2007, The Star-Ledger reported on a milestone in my life. "$400,000 ends ex-trooper's secret retaliator's suit," read the headline. The news reporter raised issue with the state's investigative tactics into the Lords of Discipline and noted that the state Attorney General's Office had doled out a settlement to me.

More important was the fact that the article detailed my allegations and commentary about the Lords. New Jersey's prominent newspaper was telling the public a story it needed to hear.

The attorney general's office, wanting to say as a little as possible, simply affirmed that the settlement was "fair and reasonable."

Newspaper Headlines

As we expected, a media domino effect ensued. Other journalistic venues—newspapers, magazines, radio, television, Internet—picked up the story of a state that would pay a trooper a considerable sum to compensate for its bullying of him, while claiming there was no ongoing problem about the bullying. The facts were given, and the public was left to decide where the truth lay. Common sense, I always believed, was our best witness.

Outrage began to mount as the state surpassed the $1,000,000 mark to settle harassment lawsuits filed by troopers. After decades of cover-up and denial, the blue wall of silence had been breached. Would the opening last, or would the forces of ignorance patch it up and move on?

The phone calls, cards and letters, and e-mails began to come— old friends from high school, relatives, people I hadn't heard from in years, all wanting me to know they saw my name in the New York Times, an Associated Press article, or heard it on television. It was great to hear from them, but it was also good to have an idea of how effective the publicity had been.

Detective Everson also reached out to me. Everson, who had retired to a rural town near the Canadian border, boasted that he was "damn proud" of me. There were state troopers who contacted me, too, and those words of appreciation meant the most of all. They wanted to express their thanks that someone had stood up and challenged things that needed challenging. I realized again just how many good men and women wear their badges, serve us daily, and have no part in the culture of corruption that stains their name and their values. But not everyone has the personal constitution or the opportunity to make a stand. If I'd had a wife and a family, for example, it would have been much more difficult to stand firm.

But there's strength in numbers, and in the simple reminder, from time to time, of why we entered the field of law enforcement in the first place. I hope that my struggle with the Lords of Discipline serve as a reminder and a wake-up call, so that perhaps, in some future day, no one will have to walk the path I followed.

So the news cycle passed, and the months passed as well. To my deep satisfaction, life grew quiet and calm. Again, I thought: *a clean conscience makes a soft pillow.* I now settled into a new career in a new state. It was exciting to become my own employer, but it was also a bit daunting. I was definitely going to thrive or fail based on my own accomplishments; there is no office politics for someone who is his own boss. So I was happy to trade the security and benefits of my old career for the freedom and incentive of a new one.

Occasionally I wondered about the New Jersey State Police, and I checked the Internet or talked to old friends to try and gauge whether anything had really changed since the news of the settlement had made the rounds. People I trusted told me that, since my case, the Lords of Discipline had fallen silent, and no one seemed to have felt their intimidating presence. The state could deny they existed and say there was no pattern of injustice, but eventually, a string of costly settlements, early retirements, and suspensions will leave a mark. Somewhere, behind closed doors, there had to have been furtive and confidential conversations occurring. I could just imagine the words: *Don't put us in this position again, boys. We've bailed you out this time, but there'd better not be a next time.*

Have the Lords disbanded? It's impossible to know for certain, but I have a hard time believing they have. There were simply too many of them ingrained in the state police culture. They are experienced officers, and in some cases (as I discovered to my shock) they are the very ones who train the rookies. If the Lords stopped existing today, it wouldn't be long before some other negative influence would move in to fill the gap. We can't hope to eliminate this kind of behavior, but we can certainly create an atmosphere that makes it less likely to exert real power.

That's what I believe we accomplished. I was certainly the face of this reform cause, but many other people were part of it. In looking back, I would describe myself as an ordinary cop with an extraordinary cause. I make no excuses and offer no apologies for being stubborn and refusing to tolerate certain actions that would have violated my oath, my integrity, and the trust of our citizenry. There are certain things in life that one could say should never be compromised, and that's the ultimate message that I hope these chapters convey.

Life, in my opinion, is composed of a thousand little instances of give-and-take every single day. To live in society we must make small sacrifices in order to gain small goals. It's true of marriage, of living in a neighborhood, or of joining a church. There are ways that we do things together, and it's impossible to do so harmoniously without these compromises.

Inevitably there are principles beneath our subtle negotiations— ideas and values that ultimately govern whether our community is a good and healthy one or not. We all have to decide on the points at which we can no longer make compromises.

I also have standards of conduct based on my foundational values concerning life: honesty, fairness, and justice. Though I'm self-employed today, I still work for those who hire my services, and they find out that all my work is guided by ethical principles. If you want me to break any laws or do anything dishonorable, you'll need to hire someone else.

Let's flip the script for a moment what about your life? Where do you make compromises, and where must you take a stand? I want people to know a couple of truths about the journey of integrity. First, it can be very lonely and discouraging. So be prepared. Second, it's ultimately more than worth it. There is so much to gain by holding out for truth, honesty, and the right way to do things. Yes, you'll pay a certain price, but you'll receive a higher reward. You will sleep better at night, you'll feel better about your life as you grow older, and the world will be a better place for your having lived in it.

On the other hand, you could be like some troopers I knew. They respected my actions; they detested the Lords of Discipline and wished they could help to wage the war against them. But in the end, they looked away and went on supporting—if only with their silence—the corruption that was occurring all around them. It weighed on me to see other young troopers with good intentions, who quickly caved in and succumbed to the pressure to compromise his values that should have been non-negotiable.

The path of simply going with the flow, of looking the other way, is not a courageous one. That person feels she is avoiding the painful price, but in fact she is paying one that will have profound implications for her life and mental well being, as well as the world around her. In the end, he will feel the emptiness of knowing that he took the low road. She had her opportunity to leave a positive imprint in this world, and she simply looked away.

My friend, don't ever let anyone tell you that fighting for integrity is a losing battle. I say the very reverse is true; giving in to it makes a loser of anyone. Don't listen to those who claim that one person can't make a difference. Human history is a record of astounding differences made by committed, uncompromising individuals.

And keep this is mind: You are one face in a crowd. You are thinking, *What can just one person possibly do?* If you could read minds, you would find that everyone else in that sea of humanity is thinking exactly the same thing. You are *not* "just one person" as long as you have so many others around you. While one person can actually do a great deal, the greater truth is that you should all be talking among yourselves and asking each other this far better question: "What can all of us do together?"

There is strength in numbers. Our entire democracy is based upon the idea that when we come together as a caring community, there is almost nothing we cannot accomplish, no shining goal we cannot reach, and no ugly social stain we cannot eradicate. If you see things that should not be happening in your place of work, or elsewhere, you can take a stand, even if it's just you against the world.

But you can also reach out to a like-minded colleague and say, "Will you join with me? Let's stand against this together."

Watch out, because once you do that, you may start a movement. You may create a landslide of reform, because so many of us yearn for a greater world, a world where our leaders don't push their sins under the carpet and live in denial. This world is waiting for one person—just one person—to refuse to give in to the sad facts of how life is, but commit himself to the inspiring possibilities of what it can be.

Will you be that person?

Epilogue:

From the Mountain Top

There was one other "exit interview" while I was still in New Jersey, recovering from my accident and preparing to move on to a new way of life. This one had no formal or required interview—it was a chance to have lunch with a pivotal influence in my life, Frank Serpico.

The author with Frank Serpico

We had spoken over the phone for a year, but I really coveted the opportunity to meet him face to face and see what the real man was like. He was kind enough to agree to a meeting, so we decided on getting together in a small town in the Catskill Mountains of New York, northwest of New York City. The Catskills make for a historic destination for tourists, who come to escape the frantic pace of the Big Apple, and to see the quaint Dutch settlements written about by Washington Irving. It's a bit different now, of course, but still a nice place to get away.

In the center of the town where we met, Serpico and I sat at an organic café and ordered lunch. We enjoyed the casual atmosphere and began talking. Several hours later, the conversation was still going.

He's a spry and lively fellow for a man in his seventies who once had to cross the ocean for a lengthy period of physical recovery. His voice is raspy, if not in the patented Al Pacino raspy. I did most of the listening, soaking up his personal story as well as his philosophies of life, law enforcement, and politics. I found that his views were all his own, transcending anyone's neat categories. Frank Serpico had been around long enough, and taken enough hard knocks, that he knew exactly what he thought about things. When you meet someone like that, it's best to simply stop and listen. You can't help but pick up a good bit of practical wisdom.

Within the hour, we were shooting a little pool in a billiard hall, and then checking out the local art exhibits together. We strolled quietly through town, enjoying the people and the mountain ambience. Later we came to a white convertible coupe. Serpico invited me to climb in, and soon we were hurtling over mountain roads. The breeze rushed by, and so did the speed limit signs. I was glad I had no credentials to ticket him!

With an unlit cigar protruding from his mouth, Serpico pointed a finger into the air, gripping the wheel with the other hand. "Know what kind of bird that is?" he asked, with a sideways glance in my direction.

I looked up to see what he was talking about. "A hawk?" I guessed.

"No, Justin," he replied. "It's a buzzard. He flies along the roadway in search of road kill."

"Really?" I smiled. "Well, you learn something every day."

I thought about how these two cops had refused to become road kill. I had to hope the buzzards had flown away by now.

It was time for dinner soon, and we shared that meal as well. I couldn't help but reflect on the differences between the two of us—in generation, in background, and in temperament. With all the things that made us distinct, the one factor bonded us. We had stood alone to fight corruption against bureaucratic machines that would not abide change, no matter how healthy the change or how expensive the refusal.

When we parted ways with a hug and a handshake, it had been a long and enlightening day—almost surreal, actually, reformers past and present, high in the mountain air, acting as old friends who had shared so much, though we had never met face to face, and were of such different ages. There's something about mountaintop experiences—something conducive to getting the long view of the past you've lived, and the future road you hope to follow. Serpico had left me with a handwritten note that read, "Interesting, looking at the world from the same place. Enjoy the view and stay focused." I was reluctant to leave the mountain where such a great sight was possible.

Driving home, I thought about my life with a full heart. I knew that I carried a few bruises, on the inside and the outside, but it was all worthwhile.

Will I be the wise and philosophical old mentor some day, like Frank Serpico? I thought. *Will people read my words, or hear my story, and find the courage to do what needs to be done?*

Who could tell? Nobody but God knows things like that. All I knew was that it was time to come down from the mountain; time to take a new road. I couldn't say exactly what lay ahead for me, but I knew I was ready to face it; ready to give myself to it; ready to stay focused, to enjoy the view, and to taste a little bit of life on the other side of the blue wall.

About the Author

Justin Hopson served as a New Jersey State Trooper before retiring in 2007.

As a trooper, Justin Hopson investigated fatal accidents, domestic violence incidents, sexual assaults, child abuse, missing persons, homicides, suicides, narcotics, and drunk driving cases. Most notably, he spearheaded the 1979 cold case investigation of Karen Zendrosky, a missing teenager who was allegedly murdered and never found. Mr. Hopson coordinated federal, state, and municipal agencies such as the National Center for Missing and Exploited Children and NecroSearch International to assist by searching for the victim's remains. As a result of moving the aforementioned case forward, he received multiple commendations and was later selected to the State Governmental Security Bureau.

While working in the State Governmental Security Bureau, Justin Hopson provided security for New Jersey's Governor, state property, and state employees within the State Capitol Complex. He was responsible for supervising, evaluating, and training the state's proprietary guard force. He provided protective services to state agencies such as the Department of Health and Agriculture, Department of Labor, and the Department of Education. Mr. Hopson was selected and trained as the NCIC Terminal Agency Coordinator (TAC) for the State Governmental Security Bureau.

As coordinator, Justin Hopson supervised and monitored state troopers' criminal history checks and NCIC 2000 inquiries. He was responsible for tracking sex offenders, missing persons, stolen guns, and wanted persons. He is technically sound in both the Amber Alert program and the LiveScan fingerprint system.

Justin Hopson holds a Master of Arts degree in management and has a high degree of professional training. Training such as gang awareness, management evaluation, and critical first response has honed his proficiency. Mr. Hopson has been certified as a State Police Instructor and American Heart Association Healthcare Provider.

As a New Jersey State Trooper, Justin Hopson diligently exposed government and police corruption. His efforts to reform government have been supported by the likes of Senator John Adler, Dr. Susan Lipkins, Frank Serpico, and the National Whistleblower Center. ABC News, The New York Times, The Philadelphia Inquirer, The Star-Ledger, and other media outlets have interviewed Mr. Hopson about police reform. Justin Hopson has successfully testified in federal, state, and municipal court proceedings.

After retiring Mr. Hopson founded Hopson Investigations, a state licensed private investigative firm based in Charleston, SC. In 2009, Justin Hopson was appointed to the Charleston County Alcohol and Drug Abuse Advisory Board. In 2010, he became a member of the South Carolina Association of Legal Investigators. These days, Justin enjoys the slow pace, sweet tea, and steepled skyline of his favorite city ~ Charleston, South Carolina.

CPSIA information can be obtained at www.ICGtesting.com
Printed in the USA
LVOW101335121211

259027LV00001B/12/P